CHINA IN
THE 21st CENTURY

LONG-TERM GLOBAL
IMPLICATIONS

ORGANISATION FOR ECONOMIC CO-OPERATION AND DEVELOPMENT

China in the 21st century   ONOMIC CO-OPERATION
ELOPMENT

Pursuant to Article 1 of the Convention signed in Paris on 14th December 1960, and which came into force on 30th September 1961, the Organisation for Economic Co-operation and Development (OECD) shall promote policies designed:

- to achieve the highest sustainable economic growth and employment and a rising standard of living in Member countries, while maintaining financial stability, and thus to contribute to the development of the world economy;
- to contribute to sound economic expansion in Member as well as non-member countries in the process of economic development; and
- to contribute to the expansion of world trade on a multilateral, non-discriminatory basis in accordance with international obligations.

The original Member countries of the OECD are Austria, Belgium, Canada, Denmark, France, Germany, Greece, Iceland, Ireland, Italy, Luxembourg, the Netherlands, Norway, Portugal, Spain, Sweden, Switzerland, Turkey, the United Kingdom and the United States. The following countries became Members subsequently through accession at the dates indicated hereafter: Japan (28th April 1964), Finland (28th January 1969), Australia (7th June 1971), New Zealand (29th May 1973), Mexico (18th May 1994), the Czech Republic (21st December 1995) and Hungary (7th May 1996). The Commission of the European Communities takes part in the work of the OECD (Article 13 of the OECD Convention).

Publié en français sous le titre :

LA CHINE AU XXIᵉ SIÈCLE
IMPLICATIONS GLOBALES A LONG TERME

Foreword

China is emerging as a major player in the world economic arena. It accounts for one-fifth of the earth's population, and a significant share of global output. With trade and production expanding at double-digit rates, the implications for many international markets as well as for the global system of trade and investment in the next century are quite daunting. So, too, are the policy challenges facing both China and the international community, for there is much to be gained from a smooth, successful integration of this huge country into the world economy.

With these prospects in mind, the OECD organised a Forum for the Future conference early in 1996. The aim was to provide an opportunity for key players in government, business, industry and research, from OECD and non-OECD countries, to assess some of the key economic and social challenges facing China over the next 15-20 years and to consider the implications and most appropriate options both for China and the international community.

The conference consisted of four sessions. The first provided a general overview of the structural and other economic and social challenges facing China, using scenarios to explore what the key issues may be in the development of the Chinese economy. The second session focused more directly on Chinese industry, in particular its likely long-term evolution in terms of labour-intensive manufacturing and high-tech production. The third examined the prospects for agriculture and energy in China, highlighting the importance of structural factors, potential supply and demand imbalances, and the possible implications for the international economy. The final session explored economic issues of a more systemic nature associated with China's emergence, and sought to identify areas of policy action that hold mutual interest for both China and the international community.

This publication brings together the papers presented at the meeting as well as an introductory contribution by the Secretariat. The book is made available on the responsibility of the Secretary-General of the OECD.

Table of Contents

China in the Twenty-first Century: An Overview of the Long-term Issues

by

Wolfgang Michalski, Riel Miller and Barrie Stevens
OECD Secretariat, Advisory Unit to the Secretary-General

In just one decade and a half, China has transformed itself from a dormant, intro-spective giant into a dynamic powerhouse of major potential significance to the world economy. Output has expanded at an average rate of nearly 10 per cent – and total exports at 17 per cent – per year. With an estimated one-fifth of the world's population, China now accounts for almost 4 per cent of world merchandise trade and a substantial share of global production (between 3 and 10 per cent, depending on whether current official exchange rates or purchasing power parities are used, and on which set of commodity price data is applied to calculate purchasing power).

This is a remarkable accomplishment by any standards. It is the fruit of a strategy, initiated in 1978, to embark on far-reaching economic liberalisation and to integrate China into the world economy. Following the success of experiments with market reforms, most notably in the agricultural sector, China's door has swung further open with greater exposure of the economy to foreign investors and freer trade in special geographical zones. A sustained series of reforms have ensued, the most recent of which are the declared intentions of the Chinese Government to allow convertibility of the currency well ahead of schedule; to step up reforms of state-owned enterprises (SOEs); and to press ahead vigorously with tariff reductions.

The reforms have been able to build on and interact with a range of critical inputs. Levels of literacy among the workforce were high, which in turn helped to engineer the substantial productivity gains of the last ten to fifteen years. China is also relatively rich in natural resources, with particularly large reserves of coal. The agricultural foundations were strong and reforms quickly led to rising farm incomes which permitted higher rates of saving among the rural population in the first years of reform. Indeed, high household saving rates helped to sustain the high investment rates (around 40 per cent of GDP in the early 1990s) on which rapid growth continues to feed. Massive inflows of foreign direct investment (FDI), though comprising only a small portion of total capital formation, have proved an important source of foreign technology and improved management techniques.

Together with rapidly expanding exports, they have also brought access to overseas markets and much-needed foreign exchange.

Thus, the foundations for continued expansion of the Chinese economy appear to be in place. Even if rates of output and export growth were to fall somewhat below current rates in the coming years, China still seems destined to become one of the world's largest (if not the largest) economy sometime in the next century. According to some projections, its level of output (although not its living standards or technological development) could become comparable to that of the United States within the next few decades.

I.   China's future: economic and social development scenarios

There is no single predetermined route for China's rise to economic pre-eminence. The external environment will doubtlessly play an important part in shaping the Chinese economy, and the handling of the reform process will be a critical factor on the domestic front. But equally, or perhaps more importantly, China faces an impressive range of structural challenges whose resolution will have a significant bearing on the size, profile and functioning of the Chinese economy fifteen to twenty years hence. Broadly speaking, these structural challenges fall into four groups: infrastructural; technological and organisational; environmental; and institutional.

Infrastructural deficiencies are likely to prove important stumbling blocks to China's economic development. It is estimated that bottlenecks in transport already cost around 1 per cent of GDP, and little improvement is foreseen given that between the 1980s and early 1990s investment in transport infrastructure declined from 1.7 to 1.0 per cent of GDP. Similarly, demands on energy production will rise substantially. Electricity generation, for example, could grow at up to 6 to 7 per cent per year to 2010. In terms of financial infrastructure, the difficulty is that while China has emerged as a major player on global financial markets, its domestic capital markets, banking sector and financial services are underdeveloped.

The volume of capital inputs is unlikely to pose a problem in the coming years, provided that saving rates hold up. But if China is to move up the specialisation ladder, away from simple labour-intensive products towards more sophisticated high-quality goods involving a wide range of advanced technologies and industries, considerable investment in human resources is likely to be required over the next ten to twenty years to secure the necessary indigenous scientific and technological foundations, the broad skill base, and the organisational know-how. Similarly, China will face the task of feeding 1.2 to 1.4 billion people, whose nutritional behaviour will in all probability change dramatically as incomes rise. Thus in the agricultural sector as well, considerable efforts will be required on all three fronts – technological, educational, and organisational.

Even at rates of growth slower than those currently recorded, China faces serious environmental problems. Most of the costs of pollution are borne by the Chinese themselves: for example, only about 20 per cent of industrial waste and 15 per cent of sewage flowing into China's rivers is treated. There is also considerable cross-border pollution, mainly due to the heavy reliance on coal and to the related carbon and sulphur emissions.

The Chinese Government has made substantial efforts since the early 1980s to reduce environmental damage. Investment in pollution prevention and control increased from virtually nil to about 1 per cent of national income towards the end of the decade. But given the prospect of continuing population pressures, rapid industrialisation, a tripling of power generation (from 150 GW in 1991 to 430 GW in 2010), and a doubling of car ownership by the end of this century, China's environmental challenge will pervade every sector of the economy.

Finally, there are institutional challenges to be confronted. For example, the current legal framework is not well adapted to a rapidly expanding, increasingly market-based and internationalising economy. Corruption is widespread. Continuing reform of state-owned enterprises implies that the social functions and responsibilities they hitherto assumed will need replacing by alternative approaches to health, education, pensions, housing and unemployment. Moreover, considerable effort will need to go into maintaining an appropriate balance between the powers and resources of the centre and the provinces. Many of the latter have, during the reform years, increased their ability to determine their own economic strategies, often quite independently of the views and wishes of central government.

Depending on the interplay of external conditions and domestic structural and policy factors in the development of the Chinese economy, overall outcomes could differ significantly.

For example, an optimistic scenario could be constructed based both on a strengthening market orientation of the Chinese economy as the authorities press ahead with economic reforms, and on a quite favourable external economic and political environment. Growth rates continue along the current long-term trajectory of around 9 per cent per annum for output and several percentage points higher for exports. These rates are sustained for quite some time, supported by high levels of domestic saving and investment – including FDI – as well as by an international economy that is willing to absorb the flood of mainly labour-intensive manufactures. This continued high-export growth is possible because China itself, after making further progress on import liberalisation, is importing goods and services of a similar order of magnitude. Significant amounts of domestic and foreign funds can be allocated to the expansion and more efficient operation of transport and energy infrastructures, thus reducing bottlenecks. Moreover, low trade barriers coupled with foreign investment and equity participation serve to stimulate competition on domestic markets. Strong growth helps to accommodate much of the surplus rural labour moving to industrial and urban areas, alleviates the repercussions of agricultural and SOE reforms, and provides revenues for environmental improvements. The widening of regional disparities within the country slows as the growth process spills over into less-developed provinces providing inputs into the coastal growth poles. Microeconomic reforms, particularly price reforms and other regulatory changes, are managed successfully, thus avoiding overheating, volatile fluctuations in macroeconomic performance and swings in policy.

A different scenario emerges from a combination of a less favourable external environment and a stalled domestic economic liberalisation process. On the external front, China's labour-intensive export drive runs into two major problems. First, OECD countries react with hostility to the assault on their textile, clothing, footwear and other affected industries. Secondly, the newly industrialising economies (NIEs) in the Asia region react negatively to the penetration of their domestic markets, and to the competition on their export markets from rival Chinese products. Export growth rates fall below output growth rates, depressing output, aggravating adjustment pressures and creating internal tensions which slow the reform process. With the sharp drop in output growth (to, say, around 4 to 5 per cent) and especially in export growth, the domestic problems begin to pile up. There is insufficient expansion in economic activity to absorb rising unemployment and establish social security systems, so that reform of agriculture and SOEs grinds to a halt. Partly as a consequence, reforms in public finances and the banking system also stall. Inflationary pressures begin to build up again and have to be tackled by price controls and other administrative measures, which in turn generate a phase of stop-go macroeconomic policies that undermine confidence in the economic climate. Lack of funding for infrastructure projects renders bottlenecks and environmental problems increasingly troublesome. Meanwhile, the depressive effect of slower export expansion on high-growth regions is magnified for the less-developed provinces, whose inhabitants see their living standards fall sharply. Social unrest follows and the liberalisation process suffers a further setback.

A third scenario can be built on the assumption of a favourable external environment but mixed success in the domestic reform process. Exports continue to grow at a brisk pace, albeit largely to the benefit of fast-industrialising coastal areas, so that regional disparities in the level of development and prosperity continue to grow apace. Infrastructure is not expanded quickly enough either to facilitate the integration of regions or to avoid bottlenecks. The reform of SOEs advances but leads to substantial dislocation of employment, which is exacerbated by large internal rural-to-urban migratory flows resulting from rapid productivity advances in agriculture. Freed-up prices and supply bottlenecks feed inflationary pressures, making management of the macroeconomy increasingly difficult. Social tensions lead the government to concentrate on the issues of widening spatial and social disparities, mass unemployment and overheating, and as a result bureaucratic policies gain ground. The economy continues to grow, but at rates in the region of only 5 to 6 per cent.

These scenarios serve to illustrate a range of crucial issues relating to China's future. Perhaps most importantly, they raise the questions of the sustainability of China's economic growth, and the role that would be played by the external environment. Is the optimistic scenario too unrealistic? Would a more hostile international trade and investment climate prove a more severe restraint on growth than the relevant scenarios suggest? The prevailing view seems to be that over the coming decade or so, economic growth rates are likely to remain in the high range, *i.e.* around 8 per cent a year. Any marked slowdown in economic activity would have important implications, not least for the labour market. Perkins spells out in the next chapter the risks of mass unemployment, with all that this would imply for social peace. A further critical issue is that of regional cohesion. There is concern that continuing high growth could exacerbate regional disparities in China. Equally, however, there is the possibility that with further progress in economic reform, the prosperity of the more successful regions may spill over into the less-developed ones, bringing important and widespread economic and social benefits.

II. China's industrial revolution: prospects for structural change in manufacturing

A range of factors will determine the future pace and character of China's ongoing industrial revolution. The primary element is the continued importance of encouraging competitive market conditions across many if not most products, types of firm, industrial sectors and regions. Progress towards more fully competitive market conditions will involve considerable structural change. However, as OECD Member countries have long recognised, facilitating structural change – even where markets have long been the tradition – usually requires significant policy reform. China is no exception. As with OECD countries, two general areas of structural change, and (therefore) sustained policy reform, will shape future prospects for Chinese industry. First, on the demand side, there are structural changes in the domestic and international markets for Chinese industrial goods. And secondly, on the supply side, there is the challenge of change in the structure, composition and factor mix of the manufacturing sector.

The overall prospects for growth in China's domestic consumer and export markets for manufactured goods are positive. Growing incomes will provide a general underpinning for dynamic demand. The specific composition and technological sophistication of this demand for manufactured items will depend on such things as the rate at which Chinese people move to the city, begin to live in larger apartments, commute further to work, gain higher average levels of education, and begin to use consumer credit. Interconnected structural changes will play a role as well, since demand for items such as furnishings, home appliances and automobiles may be constrained by prices for housing and food. However, even if China faces a situation where structural factors somewhat constrain consumer demand, it is highly likely that the domestic market for mass-produced, technologically advanced consumer goods will provide a powerful foundation for the growth of labour-intensive producers in township and village enterprises, SOEs and joint ventures. For example, meeting the demand for vehicles is expected to push the output of domestic suppliers from 1.2 million cars and trucks in 1994 to between 3 and 6 million by the end of the first decade of the next century.

In export markets China will probably continue to build on its past industrial strength and shift a greater proportion of output towards more technologically sophisticated – if still labour-intensive – products. It is widely expected that China will, if global conditions are conducive, be a major player on world markets for a broad range of technologically advanced goods, from televisions to machine tools. Lured in part by China's immense domestic market, joint ventures by export-oriented foreign multinationals will provide a strong base for China's global reach. The pace of the trend towards higher-value-added, export-oriented production will depend, in part, on the level of success in addressing various organisational and transportation constraints. For instance, at the organisational level, large-scale SOEs show very low outsourcing ratios for component procurement: 11 per cent in 1991. In contrast, outsourcing by rural township and village enterprises was over 39 per cent in the same year. Manufacturing supply networks that reach into the hinterland may create a strong demand for intermediate goods, but the cost competitiveness of such a strategy will depend on China's capacity to upgrade its telecommunications and transportation networks. Upgrading the phone system, for instance, is expected to require more than double the number of installed circuits, from 61 million in 1994 to 140 million by the year 2000.

On the assumption that Chinese exports will continue to grow at roughly the same rate as in the reform period, and overall global trade growth continues to maintain its average for the past fifteen years, China could account for over 6 per cent of the world's merchandise trade by 2010. In this type of scenario, the evolution of China's trade basically parallels previous experience with Japan and the NIEs. By 2010, China's position in world merchandise trade would be close to Japan's share in 1980 and considerably less than the NIEs' share in 1990. Attaining this trajectory will call for considerable although not insurmountable adjustments both within and outside China, particularly in specific sectors such as clothing, furniture, textiles and recording equipment. The crucial issue then becomes the likely reaction of OECD countries – but also of China's neighbouring Asian economies – to the pressures to adjust to rising manufactured exports from China.

On the supply front, China's labour, capital and technological resources and raw materials provide a powerful underpinning for long-term industrial expansion. Effective use of these endowments will hinge on important changes to allocative conditions, particularly the degree of flexibility of both prices and sources of supply in factor markets. China's diverse raw material and intermediate input markets such as steel, coal and plastics will therefore face considerable challenges in responding to industrial growth rates. If appropriate pricing and hard budget constraints are not introduced, similar difficulties can be expected for infrastructural inputs such as electricity, telecommunications and transportation.

Labour supply is generally seen as one of the main long-run sources of comparative advantage for Chinese industry. Almost regardless of the future structure of demand, China is expected to continue to specialise in labour-intensive manufacturing. What is less certain is how the structural rigidities that limit labour mobility and outsourcing to more remote, labour surplus regions will shape the development of local labour markets, especially in high-growth coastal regions. In addition, as Cable argues in a later chapter of this volume, managerial and technological skills are expected to be at a premium. Strategic use of joint ventures, FDI and policy measures such as technology zones may serve to meet much of the demand for operational, financial and technical expertise.

However, two risks cloud future prospects for adequate supplies of skilled labour. First, there will likely be intense competition for qualified personnel among the many pressing and profitable projects outside the industrial sector, particularly in the realm of large-scale infrastructure. Secondly, the formation of high-quality managerial and technical talent is significantly influenced by the corporate governance and legal frameworks within which firms are created and subjected to the rigours of the market's verdict. Future development of a strong human capital base in China will depend not only on the public (or even private) education system, but also on bankruptcy, ownership and legal reforms that create effective managerial incentive systems.

Developments in China's business services, particularly in financial, accounting and technological (*e.g.* computer and engineering) areas will also play a key role in developing managers and shaping the pace and composition of industrial growth. China already benefits from effective partnerships with firms from around the world and especially the network of Asian financial centres that serve as both suppliers and competitors. Further financial sector and banking reform will help firms put internal capital allocation on a more strategic footing, *e.g.* direct the high domestic savings to the most efficient uses. SOE reform aimed at reducing the balance sheet problems of the banking sector would also help set the stage for the development of more efficient capital markets.

Finally – as Yoshitomi points out in his contribution to this book – the pace and structure of industrial growth will be shaped by China's capacity to introduce reforms that take advantage of its relatively strong base in heavy manufacturing. Freeing up factor market prices and modernising corporate legal systems will enable allocative decisions to exploit past investments in technology and human capital so that Chinese industry can continue to move up the ladder of technological sophistication. Other supportive policies meant to encourage domestic technical and scientific achievement are already bearing fruit in places like Beijing's "Silicon Valley". In the longer term, wider and deeper forms of collaboration with foreign firms and investors that provide additional technical and financial resources will further enhance the competitive capacity of Chinese industry.

Assuming that China can achieve a relatively stable transition of its domestic economy and excluding a major breakdown of the world trading system, it is likely that the framework needed to manage the structural changes of the next two decades will emerge. Perhaps the most important issue in this context is the continuation of policy reforms towards competitive product, capital and labour markets, where prices reflect scarcities and set incentives to innovate and invest in human and physical capital. Well-functioning markets supported by a reliable legal system do more than underpin the process of structural adjustment. They also contribute to the stabilization of the economy at the macro level and enhance and broaden the economic growth potential more generally.

III. The outlook for agriculture, energy and minerals markets

The sheer size of China's economy, its rapid growth and its increasing integration into the world economy make it a crucial player in the future development of world markets for raw materials.

Chinese agriculture stands before quite daunting challenges. The country's population of 1.2 billion will increase by 200 million by 2010, and by a further 300 million by 2025; the trend to urbanisation is set to continue; and per capita incomes are likely to rise by between 2.5 and 4.5 per cent annually. All of this can be expected to bring about important changes in food consumption patterns. While per capita demand for grain (*i.e.* rice and cereals) for direct consumption will decline, per capita intake of meat and fish is expected to at least double over the next fifteen years. This dietary shift to animal products will put considerable pressure on feed grain demand. (Metabolic conversion of cereals in animals is poor: it takes 2 kilograms of feed grain to produce 1 kilogram of poultry; pork requires 4 kilograms; beef needs 7 kilograms.) The net result is that total demand for grain could increase from its present level of about 400 MMT (million metric tonnes) to well over 500 MMT by 2010 and close to 600 MMT by 2020.

A key concern is whether China – with 22 per cent of the world's population yet only 7 per cent of the arable land – will be able to meet this surge in grain demand. There have been serious losses of arable land to non-farm uses in recent years; environmental degradation of land and shortages of water are becoming increasingly critical – both are partly due to underpriced synthetic fertilizers and irrigation water supplies priced at a fraction of actual costs; inefficiencies and delays during harvesting, threshing, drying, storage and transport account for annual losses of an estimated 60-100 MMT of grain; and investment in agricultural research fell sharply during the 1980s, thereby weakening the basis for further productivity gains (at least over the medium term). As a result, the more pessimistic forecasters predict a substantial shortfall in China's grain supplies over the next twenty years or so, which in the worst case could, by the end of the projection period, be in the range of 100 to 200 MMT. On the other hand, due to under-reporting, farmland areas and in some cases yields are probably substantially larger than the official records suggest; yields of some major crops are still below global averages and there is also a huge potential for yield increases through crop specialisation across the various regions of China; losses during harvest, storage and transport could be considerably reduced; and finally, significant efficiency gains could be expected from higher investment in agricultural research and irrigation. More moderate estimates – such as that by Lin, Huang and Rozelle in this volume – put the likely annual shortfall in grain (mainly wheat) at about 40 MMT.

China possesses the world's third largest coal reserves, and it is mainly on these that the economy will rely for its energy supplies in the coming decades. Primary coal demand (which currently accounts for more than two-thirds of total primary energy demand) is expected to increase at a rate of over 3 per cent a year to satisfy rising industrial output growth and mounting demand for electricity. As in agriculture, the question arises whether China has the capacity to meet this demand with domestic supplies. Raising output to adequate levels will involve substantial investment in the modernisation of existing mines and new coal mine development, much of which will take time to come on stream. If, in the meantime, economic growth continues at 8 to 9 per cent, there is a possibility that demand for coal could eventually outstrip supply, even after recourse to stockpiles. If, in addition, bottlenecks in rail transport were to intensify (coal accounting for 40 per cent of rail freight) and/or the cost of extracting the coal were to rise significantly above world prices, China's position could change from that of net exporter to net importer of coal.

With the widely anticipated expansion of road traffic (both passenger and freight), the most rapid growth in Chinese energy demand is expected to be in oil. Passenger kilometres, for example, are foreseen to more than quadruple between 1991 and 2010. According to the projections in Priddle's chapter, demand could surge over the next fifteen years from its current level of about 3 million barrels per day (mb/d) to around 6.5 mb/d, implying imports by 2010 of about 2.8 mb/d, an increasing proportion of which could be coming from Middle East suppliers. Faster, more effective exploitation of potentially important oil fields, such as in the remote, hostile environment of the Tarim Basin, could help reduce the gap by up to 1 mb/d, but there would still be a need to import (net) some 1.5 mb/d. Moreover, if domestic crude oil production costs continue to rise on recent trends, the average cost of Chinese crude oil could well overtake international market prices, casting doubt on the viability of at least some domestic exploration and extraction projects.

As in agriculture, improved efficiency and technological advances could help reduce potential domestic demand and supply imbalances significantly. In exploration and extraction of coal and oil, for example, advanced geological data processing technology could substantially boost discovery of new fields. Moreover, improvements in thermal efficiency in power generation promise substantial savings in fuel. It is estimated that at current levels of thermal efficiency (30 per cent), coal consumption in China's power sector will rise from about 390 to 1 020 million tonnes by 2010. A 5 per cent improvement in thermal efficiency would imply coal consumption of only 755 million tonnes in 2010, a saving of over 25 per cent. Foreign direct investment will be vital for technological progress in this domain.

The quest for improved energy efficiency is also closely intertwined with environmental issues. China ranks as one of the largest contributors of greenhouse gas emissions (11 per cent) in the world, and its contribution over the next twenty to thirty years will in all probability continue to be extensive. Projections put China's CO_2 emissions by the year 2025 at between 1 400 and 1 700 million tons. However, it is estimated that for every 1 per cent increase in energy efficiency in power generation, there is a reduction in CO_2 emissions of the order of 3 to 4 per cent. For both energy efficiency and the environment, pricing plays an all-important role, but most energy prices, and especially electricity tariffs, are well below economic cost. For example, average industry electricity tariffs in China in 1993 were approximately one-tenth of Japan's, less than one-third of India's, and half of Korea's. Consequently, there is little incentive to engage in energy conservation and lower emission levels (total fixed capital spending in the state-owned energy sector devoted to energy conservation investment is as low as 6 per cent).

Contrary to popular perception, China is not rich in non-fuel minerals, although there are a few exceptions. In many products, domestic Chinese ores are often remote from markets, high-cost, and of inferior quality (for instance, average iron grade is only half that of internationally traded iron ore). China's usage of minerals and metals, however, is fairly intensive. Its steel output is on a par with Japan's; it ranks among the largest producers of aluminium in the world; and it is the largest producer of tin, a sizeable zinc producer, and a major user of copper. Given China's stage of development – in which growing infrastructure needs translate into particularly intensive use of materials – it is generally expected that in the years ahead, demand for minerals and metals will outpace the rate of economic expansion.

Looking across agriculture, energy and mineral markets, the principal issue is about the implications of likely supply and demand imbalances for world markets. Without question, China is an increasingly important player in all these areas. Erratic shifts in its exports and imports arising from such factors as sharp discrete jumps in production, command-economy-type decisions, and speculative trade into and out of inventories can lead to wild fluctuations in supply and prices – at least in the short run – with significant destabilization of global markets. This is already the case with certain agricultural products (including cotton and wool) and minerals (such as copper, aluminium and zinc), and could apply also to oil in the future. Vulnerability of world oil markets could increase over the short term to the extent that sharp growth in China's imports may contribute to further reducing OPEC reserve capacities.

Potential long-term effects are also of considerable interest. With respect to grain, oil and certain key non-fuel minerals, large increases in China's imports, for example, could lead to sustained price rises. But these may prove less dramatic than expected, since there is considerable scope for expanding worldwide supply capacity and, in the case of energy and minerals, for curbing consumption, exploiting new sources and introducing substitutes. With respect to grain, for example, there is considerable under-utilised production potential in the United States, Canada, Australia, Argentina and the Ukraine – and as far as oil is concerned, it is a widely held view that capacity expansion, new extraction technologies and alternative energy sources would effectively cap prices at $25-28 per barrel. Both the problem of short-term fluctuations in supply and prices and the prospect of long-term expansion of Chinese markets focus added attention on the future of China's self-sufficiency policy, and on the kind of international policy framework that would be needed if China were to change its approach to the question of security and stability of supply, and developed greater confidence in international markets.

IV. The implications for domestic policy and international co-operation

China's continuing integration into the world economy holds considerable potential advantages both for China and for the international community. Greater openness on China's part could strengthen the country's reform efforts towards a more market-oriented economy and bring substantial benefits to its people. From an international perspective, enhanced co-operation with China across a broad range of activities is expected to generate considerable benefits for the world economy over the next decades. However, the integration process will inevitably be associated with a wide range of structural changes, not only within China itself but also in the international economy at large. What will prove vital to the smoothness of the integration process is the geographical and sectorial distribution of the costs and benefits of change as perceived by the international community.

As Chinese exports continue to grow, the spotlight is fairly certain to fall on the evolution of China's overall trade balance and balance of payments. The indications at present are that it is unlikely that China will run long-term surpluses on either. Since reforms began in the late 1970s, the Chinese economy has run both a trade deficit and a current account deficit in most years. Moreover, relatively high rates of growth will continue to absorb high domestic savings and large import volumes, the vast bulk of which will continue to be industrial goods. Machinery and transportation equipment, particularly items embodying higher levels of technology than China can produce domestically, are the fastest-growing imports. (China's total import requirements in equipment and technology to the end of this century are estimated at $100 billion annually.) However, there is also huge potential for high-value services.

Over the years, as China moves increasingly into line with its comparative advantage profile, and as the Multi-Fibre Agreement (MFA) is dismantled and the Uruguay Round agreements are implemented, the international environment may prove increasingly favourable both to China's traditional labour-intensive exports and to more sophisticated technology-intensive goods.

The impact of traditional labour-intensive exports on OECD markets should prove relatively limited. The affected sectors now account for only a small proportion of output in most Member countries, and have in any case undergone considerable streamlining in the last couple of decades under persistent competitive pressure from Asian NIEs. However, there could well be resistance from some OECD economies perhaps perceiving a greater amount of "catch-up" adjustment than is actually called for. By the same token, many of the industrialising economies in Asia and Latin America are increasingly exposed to Chinese labour-intensive exports and will need to share a large (if not the largest) part of the adjustment burden, thus lending a distinct geographic asymmetry to the global adjustment process. The potential for trade tensions between China and many of its Asian trading partners could be exacerbated if, over the coming years, the process of import liberalisation is seen to unfold much more rapidly among the NIEs and ASEAN countries than in China.

Rising Chinese exports in machinery and equipment, on the other hand, would signify a move away from inter-industry and towards intra-industry trade with OECD countries and some Asian NIEs, involving perhaps lower adjustment costs for these countries. Again, however, the differential between the pace of import liberalisation in China and that in the Asian NIEs (including in the APEC context) could prove crucial to the evolution of trading relations in the region.

In resolving potential tensions of a more systemic nature, much will depend on the speed and smoothness of the convergence of Chinese domestic methods for regulating the economy towards the rule-based functioning of the international trade regime, as well as on the degree to which China and its trading partners acknowledge and abide by the international rules of the game, however these may look fifteen to twenty years hence. An equally important factor, however, will be the willingness of both China and the international community to co-operate in tackling many of China's structural challenges – which, though less directly related to trade, will have a noticeable impact on the global economy.

China's increasing openness should prove an advantage in this regard. Notwithstanding its huge internal potential – in terms of the size of its domestic market, its high savings and abundant labour, its capacity to support a broad range of manufacturing industries, and its wealth of natural resources – China has increased its interdependence with the world economy at several levels. For example, inflows of FDI are impressive by any standards. Moreover, the country's reliance on exports produced by foreign-invested firms is greater than anywhere else in East Asia; indeed, these companies accounted for over two-thirds of China's total export growth in recent years. Outward FDI is a further manifestation of China's deepening links with the world economy. No official records are published, but it is estimated that in 1993 cumulative Chinese investment in Hong Kong alone exceeded $20 billion. And although equity markets in China are still in their infancy, foreign equity ownership is already encouraged: by 1993, foreign holdings accounted for 5 per cent of the combined capitalisation on the Shanghai and Shenzhen exchanges.

This increasing global integration of the Chinese economy enlarges rather than diminishes the scope for co-operative policy action, both on the Chinese domestic and the international fronts, in meeting the long-term structural challenges China faces. This applies in particular to the domains of technology, infrastructure, and the environment already identified in the previous sections. For example:

- China's investment requirements in transportation and telecommunications to the beginning of the next century are put at close to $170 billion, and its energy investment requirements to 2015 are thought to be in the range of $1 000 billion. These are orders of magnitude that surpass even China's considerable capital resources. The investment opportunities for businesses in OECD and non-OECD countries are therefore substantial. But it may not be easy to sustain or increase inflows of FDI and foreign participation – and thus transfers of foreign technology – into these sectors unless further progress is made not only in terms of setting appropriate incentives for investors and bringing about greater convergence in perceptions of risk, but also (and equally important) in terms of correcting deficiencies in the legal system. The latter refer to the protection of foreign investors and their investments, the transparency and predictability of rules, enforcement of law and regulations, and territorial subdivisions.
- With respect to supplies of agricultural produce, minerals, fuels and other raw materials, China faces difficult policy choices on the question of self-sufficiency. If it chooses to rely more heavily on international markets, its role in determining global prices and supply will be considerably magnified. Even if it chooses to maintain a policy of "approximate" independence, seasonal and cyclical factors will ensure that China nevertheless remains a major international player. The degree of reliance that China places on international markets will be inextricably linked to its confidence in the ability of major producers to maintain supplies, and in the global rules that govern those markets. China, for its part, as well as other actors on the international markets, could draw satisfaction from the prospect of further progress towards industrial reform and a more stable framework for macroeconomic activity, which would help to smooth out the artificial fluctuations on international commodity markets brought about in the past by abrupt swings in China's supply requirements.
- China's contribution to world greenhouse gas emissions will increase over the next twenty to thirty years. There is nonetheless abundant scope for improvement. For example, given sufficient progress in increasing thermal efficiency, China could reduce the growth of its annual CO_2 emissions by at least 130 million tonnes by 2010. Such advances, however, may only be possible through a combination of domestic and international initiatives. On the domestic front, reform of energy pricing would bring considerable environmental benefits by redressing incentives. On the international front, foreign technology will prove to be a key ingredient. Private foreign investment through FDI is one source of such technology; others are the multilateral and bilateral development assistance agencies and

international development banks. With respect to these, there is room for shifting assistance away from large-scale supply-side projects and towards schemes to promote improvements in end-use energy efficiency.

Advancing the process of China's integration into the world economy will require both its participation in institutional frameworks and mechanisms for dispute resolution such as the WTO, and moving beyond rule-making and procedural bodies to a broader set of institutions and relations. This will also imply a strong shift in emphasis away from bilateral and towards multilateral approaches such as dialogue with the OECD and possibly, in the longer term, the G7.

For China and its global partners, progressing along all of these paths will hinge on the capacity to introduce mutually reinforcing policies that build confidence and trust. It is well recognised that this requires consistent and responsible behaviour by all countries. As the measures integrating China into the world economy are put into place and its presence on the world stage grows, the stakes for all participants will be higher. China's integration into the world economy opens up the prospect of a massive new growth pole. Fulfilling this potential, in a way that benefits all countries, will depend on building a common understanding in the key areas of trade and investment, and on the wider context of shared economic and ecological responsibilities.

China's Future: Economic and Social Development Scenarios for the Twenty-first Century

by

Dwight H. Perkins
Harvard Institute for International Development

The best way to begin a speculative exploration of China's economic future over the next decade or two is with an outline of the major elements determining whether China's economic growth may be fast or slow. Various combinations of these elements may then lead to differing scenarios about the possible future course of China's economic, social and political development. From the outset, it is important to note that China's economic performance depends first on what happens to the reform process within the country. But China's external environment will also play a major role in shaping its prospects.

I.   What determines China's economic growth?

Since the reform process was initiated in December 1978, China's official GNP growth rate accelerated from around 4.5 per cent per year in the previous two decades to roughly 9 per cent per year in the subsequent seventeen years through 1995.[1] Among the elements which shaped this rapid growth were the availability of standard production inputs such as capital, foreign exchange, energy and technology; an economic system based on an efficient combination of market forces and state intervention; and sufficient control over or reduction of social tensions so that the political system had the capacity to create a stable environment for investment.

Among the critical inputs for China, capital is the most straightforward. From the early 1970s – before market-oriented reforms began – China has maintained a rate of capital formation that is above 30 per cent of net material product (NMP), reaching a peak of 38.7 per cent of NMP in 1993.[2] In the 1970s, these high rates were maintained by high government taxes that provided the funds for large investments by state-owned enterprises. Since the reforms began, tax revenues and investment from the government budget have fallen sharply, but have been offset by an equally sharp rise in private savings. For a time, some analysts believed these high savings rates were a transitory

21

phenomenon – but few hold that position today. As long as growth and profitable investment opportunities remain high, there is every reason to believe that China's rate of investment will also remain high.

Foreign direct investment (FDI) has been increasingly important in this context, with FDI actually utilised rising to $33.8 billion in 1994. Most of these funds come from Hong Kong and from Chinese living overseas, but a portion is domestic Chinese money recycled through Hong Kong to take advantage of the favourable treatment given to foreign investors. Even if the official figures are somewhat inflated, there is little doubt that China in the 1990s was by far the largest recipient of FDI in the developing world. Will this level of FDI continue, and does it matter?

Large as FDI into China has been, it is still a relatively small fraction of total Chinese investment. "Accumulation" in 1993 was 1 007 billion yuan – which, at the official exchange rate in that year, came to $175 billion. However, if instead of the official exchange rate a purchasing power parity rate is used, Chinese GDP in 1993 was over $1 800 billion, with investment in that year at around $700 billion.[3] FDI, then, was either 5 or 19 per cent of total investment, depending on which exchange rate is used. Continued high levels of FDI are thus not critical to China's ability to maintain a high overall rate of investment. FDI's importance, rather, is as a direct source of foreign exchange and, even more, as a source of advanced technology, improved management techniques, and access to foreign markets.

Foreign exchange availability was once a major constraint on Chinese economic growth. In 1978, total Chinese exports were only $9.75 billion, and before 1972 exports hovered around the $2 billion figure each year. But one of the notable successes of the reform period has been China's ability to turn itself into a major exporter of manufactures. In 1995, Chinese exports reached $150 billion, an annual rate of increase over the past seventeen years of 17 per cent in nominal terms. Since 1990 the increase rate has been 19 per cent per year, or around 15 per cent in real terms. FDI firms accounted for 29 per cent of exports in 1994. Hong Kong, from which much of the FDI comes, handled over half of all Chinese manufactured exports, largely because of its formidable marketing skills.

One central question for the future is whether export growth rates of anything like this magnitude can continue – and if they cannot do so, will that create problems for China's growth prospects? Growth rates of 15 per cent per year in real terms are not very likely on a long-term basis; they would result in China exports of $600 billion in 2005 and $2 400 billion in 2015. It is hard to imagine the world being able to accommodate such a massive increase, even if Chinese imports grew by a comparable amount. But even growth rates of 9 per cent per year would give China exports of $350 billion in 2005 and $840 billion in 2015. Rates much lower than this could mean that China's foreign trade ratio (exports plus imports divided by GNP) was falling, if GNP kept growing at rates comparable to what has occurred over the past seventeen years. China, in effect, would have to begin to turn its economy back inward if GNP were to grow at 8 or 9 per cent per year, while exports grew at only 5 or 6 per cent in real terms. Few economies in the twentieth century have tried to turn their economy back inward, and none have done so with much success in terms of maintaining a high economic growth rate.

Part of the answer to whether the world can make room for another Asian export giant comparable to Japan will turn on whether China attempts to copy Japan's mercantalist policies that, together with that country's excessive saving rate, have given Japan such a large trade surplus. Assuming China can avoid trade surpluses of that magnitude, the other principal questions will be whether the world trading system in general remains as open as it has been over the past five decades, and whether world trade in general continues to grow faster than world GNP.

If China can continue to generate large amounts of foreign exchange through exports and FDI, then shortages of particular commodities are not likely to constrain growth. With $150 billion it is possible to import large quantities of petroleum and grain. Imports of 50 million tons of grain, for example – barring a major increase in world prices – would cost under $10 billion. Imports of 2 million barrels of petroleum per day at $20 per barrel would cost China $14.6 billion. China could well have imports of this magnitude in ten years or less and world prices might rise further as a result, but if Chinese exports by then are over $300 billion, these imports would still use up only 10 per cent or less of the foreign exchange available. Energy is a constraint on Chinese economic growth, mainly because China has had difficulty keeping electric power capacity growing with the rapid increase in demand, not because of a failure to find adequate resources of petroleum or coal. And China's difficulty in keeping its power capacity up with demand has more to do with policy and management failures than with a lack of ability to pay for the necessary equipment.

Of course, China's expanding economy cannot succeed by simply churning out more textiles, toys and consumer electronics for domestic and foreign markets. Like all other currently industrialised economies, China will have to move up the ladder steadily away from simple labour-intensive products and toward areas of ever-higher technological and organisational sophistication. Does China have the human resources to accomplish this task over the next two decades?

The answer partly hinges on whether China will continue to have access to world advanced technologies through imports of advanced equipment, licences and the like. Barring a return to the cold war, China will almost certainly have such access. But the answer depends to a far greater extent on whether China's own science and technology establishment will have the capacity to make full use of these advanced technologies. "Full use" implies that Chinese industry and services will move up the technological ladder across a wide range of industries, and not just achieve world-class status in only a few sectors in order to achieve military parity. In short, is China going to accomplish what Japan did in the 1950s and 1960s, or is it going to be more like the Soviet Union in the 1970s and 1980s?

In the period between 1958 and 1978, China's leaders did enormous damage to the country's educational and research resources. A whole generation of people who would be in their prime today were deprived of an education beyond secondary school. But China's human resources were always well ahead of most countries', with a comparable level of per capita income. As with China's East Asian neighbours, Confucian values among other influences had created an elite of highly educated people long before the Communists came to power in 1949. Also like other East Asian states, China began a

23

rapid expansion of its educational system at all levels in the 1950s, and renewed this effort after 1978. For all the shortages in funding for China's universities, the quality as well as the quantity of students with the capacity to become first-rate scientists and engineers has risen rapidly. More than 100 000 of these students have been sent abroad for further degree training, and many more have gone on shorter visits to learn specific technologies. From economics to physics, some of the best Ph.D. students in American universities come from China.

One important issue is whether the Chinese students who have gone abroad will return home. Up through 1995, over 90 per cent of those who obtained advanced degrees allowing access to employment opportunities in the United States or Europe did not return to China. But over 90 per cent of the students Korea and Chinese Taipei sent abroad also did not return during the first two decades when these two economies began to grow rapidly. However, by the 1970s many students from Korea and Chinese Taipei were going home and by the 1980s most were returning, often after working for years in places like Silicon Valley. Greater economic opportunities at home were the primary draw, but the growing openness of society in the two countries also helped. The returning students became the backbone of these economies' increasingly sophisticated industries. If China becomes steadily more prosperous and its society more open, there is no reason to think that the Chinese experience will be any different. But China will have to greatly expand its university system if it is to take full advantage of its potential to become a technologically advanced nation. At present, only about 4 per cent of the 18-21 age group is enrolled in an institution of higher education – but 4 per cent is still 2.5 million students.

II. Reforming the economic system

Capital, foreign exchange and an educated population will only sustain rapid economic growth if the economic system is capable of using these resources effectively. For a quarter of a century China had a command system modelled on that of the Soviet Union, one of the most wasteful economic systems in the world. In 1978 it began to move away from that model in what, over time, came to be a systematic effort to replace commands with the market.

There are two closely related questions in determining how these reforms are likely to influence China's future economic performance. First, will China succeed in completing the transition to a market economy? Secondly, just what kind of a market economy is China transitioning toward, and will it perform as well as the Chinese leadership hopes?

China has come a long way on the road to a market economy. Agriculture is based on household production, which responds mainly to market forces. The government's role in setting farm prices is no more pervasive than it is in most other countries. There is as yet no rural land market or efficient rural capital market, but those are coming. Personal services, most retail trade, and even a large share of wholesale trade are, for all practical purposes, privatised and governed by market forces.

Even industry is increasingly market-oriented. Most industrial inputs are now sold on the market at market prices, a sharp contrast from ten years earlier. Over half of all industry is now outside the state sector, the bulk of this being the township and village enterprises (TVEs) and foreign equity joint ventures. "Outside the state sector" signifies that most of these enterprises are formal collectives with close ties to local governments. Unlike the large state-owned enterprises, however, they cannot depend on continuing subsidies from the government budget or the banking system. In the jargon of economics, they face a "hard budget constraint".

The big questions about the future of market reforms focus on the role and nature of the larger state-owned enterprises and their relationship to the financial system. The central problem with state-owned enterprises is that a large percentage of them perform poorly, primarily because of their close ties to government ministries and bureaus. Until that umbilical cord is cut they will never be truly autonomous, capable of standing on their own. Their lack of independence has also undermined the banking system, which has had the primary responsibility for keeping state enterprises afloat.

There are two major reasons why it has been difficult to reform state enterprises in China. One is that they are the main providers of many urban services, from housing to pensions to health care. If an enterprise were to go bankrupt, those dependent on it would lose their housing, their pensions, and much else. The solution is to separate these functions from the enterprise by privatising housing, or by at least making government rather than the enterprise responsible for public housing. A national pension system, national health insurance, and a national unemployment compensation scheme are also part of the solution. The Chinese are working on reforms in all of these areas, but getting from the pilot stage to full national implementation has proved difficult.

The second reason is that the government bureaucracy has been reluctant to relinquish the power and perquisites that go with their control over state enterprises. The power of patronage – the right to appoint senior enterprise management – is one example. Local governments and even the Ministry of Finance depend on the enterprises for revenue, including revenues over and above those required by the formal tax system. Anyone familiar with the experience of eastern Europe over the past two decades will understand the nature of the problem.

There are several ways in which the role of state-owned enterprises could evolve. One is that bureaucratic control from above the enterprise becomes increasingly rigid, and the current partially reformed system becomes permanent. A second is that the state succeeds in cutting state enterprises loose and many of them prove that they can compete effectively in domestic and international markets.

A third scenario, and probably the most likely, is that the state enterprises in their present form will be absorbed into new entities that behave much like private corporations in the West. This process is already under way. Most larger foreign equity joint ventures are with state enterprises – and increasingly, it is the equity joint venture that is squeezing out the pure state entity. Similar transformations are occurring in the close subcontracting ties that exist between state enterprises and the TVEs. Finally, state enterprises are increasingly converting over to shareholding systems where the shareholders do not yet have the right to hire and fire management, a prerogative that could come with time.

Even if China creates some approximation of a Western corporate structure, however, there remains the question of the intended role for the central government planners and ministries. There is no clearly articulated view on this subject in China, but many in the government bureaucracy would like to see a system patterned on that of Japan's Ministry of International Trade and Industry in the 1960s and 1970s, or Korean industrial policy under President Park in the 1970s.

The essence of the policy during President Park's heavy and chemical industry drive is that government planners decided what was to be done and then left it up to the large private conglomerates (*chaebols*) to implement the plan. If the private sector agreed to build the Blue House-planned heavy machinery complex or shipyard, the government did its best to ensure the success of the venture. The levers available to the government to carry out this task were formidable. Banks were state-owned and could be ordered to make large loans to these projects at below market interest rates. Corporate taxes were negotiable and the outcome of the negotiations often depended on the willingness of the private company to carry out the government's plan. Imports were subject to quotas and high tariffs that could be lifted for firms that co-operated.

Japan's MITI operated in much the same way. In fact, the Koreans to a degree patterned their system after Japan's, only they took it a step or two further. It is not difficult to understand the appeal of this kind of industrial policy to Chinese government bureaucrats. It creates an all-powerful economic bureaucracy not unlike the command system Chinese bureaucrats grew up with. The major difference is that in Korea, the individual enterprises carrying out the plans are more independent and hence more efficient than in the Chinese case. In contrast, enterprises in China have not had much more true autonomy than bureaus within a government ministry. Some of the Korean heavy industry enterprises, while autonomous, were not even privately owned; the highly successful steel-maker POSCO, for example, was and is a state-owned enterprise.

Could China make a government bureaucracy-dominated industrial policy work as well as the Japanese and Korean systems? There are those who argue that the government-led industrial policies in Japan and Korea did not work all that well either, but no one can seriously dispute that they worked far better than the Chinese Soviet-style command system. The Japanese and Koreans did, however, have one major advantage that is missing in the Chinese case: their economic bureaucracies were almost completely insulated from politics. They were also well isolated from forces of corruption that were very much present in Japanese and Korean society, but not a major influence on government bureaucrats. As a result, industrial policies in the two countries were made almost exclusively on technical criteria. These were not always the right criteria and mistakes were made, but the degree of error was far less than when decisions are dominated by politics and corrupt practices.

It is hard to imagine a situation where the current government bureaucracy in China – or in most developing countries for that matter – could be insulated from either politics or corruption. Chinese political leaders do not enjoy the unchallenged political bases of Japan's Liberal Democratic Party in its prime, or President Park's military/rural former constituency. Elements of the government bureaucracy are themselves part of the political base of individual Chinese leaders, and rent-seeking state corruption in China cannot be effectively controlled as long as the opportunities for rent-seeking remain so prevalent. Police work will not do the job unless China is prepared to return to the extreme policies of the past, which seems highly unlikely. Only by removing the pervasive availability of rent-seeking opportunities will corruption be brought under control.

The primary source of both rent-seeking and political influence in economic decisions is the pervasive discretionary authority of the government over these decisions. The need for licences and approvals to do almost anything in China means that every project, large or small, must weave its way through a maze of official discretionary decisions. In Japan and Korea this maze could be focused on technical goals, but it is hard to see how that degree of focus could be accomplished in China. The size of China alone makes systematic control from Beijing over these decisions an impossibility.

The way out of this dilemma is for China to abandon hope of creating a Japanese/Korean-style system and to move toward an industrialisation programme based mainly on market forces. Large parts of the licensing and control apparatus would have to be dismantled. Land and capital could be allocated at market-determined prices. International trade would have to be liberalised much further, perhaps through China's joining the World Trade Organization and abiding by its rules except for limited infant industry protection.

There would still be plenty for the government to do in the economic arena. China is not going to be a giant Hong Kong. Much large-scale infrastructure would continue to be built by the state. Laboratories for research and development would probably depend mainly on state funds. Some industries, such as the railroads and electric power, would continue to be regulated as well as owned by the state. China would have a mixed private-public system not unlike that of Korea in the 1990s. With this kind of system, there is reason to believe that China's economy would operate almost as efficiently as those of its most dynamic neighbours.

III. Social pressures and political stability

Even with high growth, the strains in Chinese society will be considerable. If growth slows markedly, those strains could escalate.

China's central social problem in the future is likely to be employment. Poverty, particularly for persons at the very bottom of the income distribution, is also an important issue, but one with less national political significance. Those below the ''poverty line'' are declining steadily in number, and the ones who remain are mostly in remote areas, far from the centres of power. That is not the case with the unemployed and underemployed.

Between 1978 and 1993, China's labour force increased by two hundred million people. Formally, almost all of these people were employed because Chinese statistics only recognise a very limited number of the registered urban population (4 to 5 million) as being formally unemployed. But 340 million members of this workforce are in farming, with only 100 million hectares of arable land – or 0.3 hectares per worker. In

1957 there were 147 million fewer workers on the same amount of land, and many were considered to be underemployed even then. The mechanisation of farming that has taken place since 1957 has made at least 150 million farmers, and possibly more, surplus to requirements. They could leave the land and they are leaving the land, without much loss in agricultural production. No one, except perhaps Chinese public security, knows the precise numbers, but it is widely believed that these surplus farmers now constitute a "floating" population of around 100 million. This floating population does much of the urban construction work, is involved in small-scale trading and services of all kinds, and moves around seeking jobs.

One of the outstanding achievements of the first decade of Chinese reforms was that a majority of all new entrants into the labour force found work outside agriculture – that is, they found productive employment as opposed to simply increasing the number of surplus farmers. Between 1978 and 1988 the workforce rose by 142 million (14 million per year), while employment in industry and services rose by 103 million. The state sector accounted for only 25 million of these jobs; the rest were generated by the collective and private sector. During the austerity years of 1989 and 1990, in contrast, the workforce rose by 24 million, but employment in industry did not rise at all while services employment rose by 6 million. The other 18 million were farmers or "floaters". With renewed growth in 1991, employment in industry and services again rose by 36 million, or over 100 per cent of the increase in the workforce. In 1992, for the first time, the number of farmers actually declined.

These numbers have been presented in order to make a simple point. If China grows rapidly at 8 or 9 per cent per year, the economy is capable of absorbing new entrants into the labour force into real jobs in industry and services. Projecting ten or twenty years into the future, high growth will absorb all of the current surplus of labour in the agricultural sector. Farm workers, who in 1993 made up 56 per cent of the workforce, would fall to under 40 per cent in 2005 and perhaps 25 per cent of the total in 2015. There would still be more farmers than needed, but China would be primarily an industrial/services/urban society.

Services will and should play a larger role in the growth of employment than industry. This statement applies to the past seventeen years, but even more to the future. In the 1980s China moved away from the command economy view that sees most services as parasitic, and encouraged some development in this sector. The share of employment in services rose from 12.1 per cent of total employment in 1978 to 21.2 per cent in 1993. The 1993 figure, however, is still far below the share of services employment elsewhere in Asia. The Republic of Korea share, for example, is 47.7 per cent, and even in the Philippines the share is 38.7 per cent. In most OECD countries the share of services in total employment is between 65 and 70 per cent.

The development of China's service sector, therefore, still has a long way to go. If the GNP growth rate remains high, the share of employment in services can be expected to rise without much direct help from policy; for sectors such as commerce, simply the absence of government interference may be sufficient. For modern service sectors such as insurance, pensions and other financial services, however, a reliable legal framework is essential, and only government is in a position to build such a framework. In the absence of a government effort to develop the institutions required by a modern service sector, employment growth and ultimately GNP growth as well will, therefore, slow down.

What if economic growth falls to 4 or 5 per cent a year and is concentrated in the large-scale state sector? There was a brief glimpse of what might happen in 1989-90 – and a longer view during the 1957-78 period, when GNP growth was around 4.5 per cent per year and less than half of the increase in the workforce found jobs outside agriculture. The 1989-90 experience was enough to alter radically the priorities of many in the Chinese leadership in a very short space of time. Vigorous critics of township and village enterprises in 1988 and 1989 became enthusiastic converts to the programme in 1991. Double-digit inflation, which had been seen as the number one economic and political problem, suddenly was no longer something that had to be dealt with at any cost. Inflation was again to double digits in 1993, and down somewhat in 1995 but still in double digits.

Slow growth, not just outright economic stagnation, means that huge numbers of people in China – tens of millions and perhaps over one hundred million – will have trouble finding work. If that situation were to combine with widespread urban discontent, it would be an explosive mixture. Ten and twenty years from now the university system will be pouring several million new graduates into the workforce each year. In 1995 there was still a great shortage of well-trained university graduates. But will university-level jobs open up at the rate required? If GNP growth is 9 or 10 per cent a year, the university system will have to expand at a rapid rate simply to keep up with demand. However, at a 4 or 5 per cent per year GNP growth, Confucian values within Chinese families may push far more students into the system than the economy can absorb.

China, like several other parts of East Asia, has a long tradition of student activism that has led to major political change dating back to the May 4 Movement of 1919. Student grievances by themselves are seldom sufficient to put major pressure on governments. But when grievance has combined with tacit or active support from large parts of the urban population, educated and otherwise, more than a few East Asian governments have fallen.

Will a future Chinese government have the power to keep the lid on these pressures? It is unlikely that the Chinese population would accept the kind of repression that existed in the 1960s and 1970s – even if leaders could be found who would be willing to try such methods. In the absence of effective repression, it is difficult to speculate about what form an explosion in social tensions might take. Eventually a new political system capable of maintaining order would evolve. Whether that order would be authoritarian or democratic cannot be known, and in any case speculation about alternative paths to political change is well beyond the scope of this essay.

In any case, political turmoil is not likely to lead to the breakup of China in a way analogous to what happened to the Soviet Union. Ninety-two per cent of the people of China are Han and think of themselves first as Chinese. With the exception of occasional periods of a decade or two when the country has been engulfed in civil wars or when foreign nomadic people conquered parts of it, China has been unified for most of the past 1 300 years.

If there is serious political disorder, therefore, it will feed back on economic policy and performance in ways that will keep economic growth low. Alternatively, if there is political stability as well as sensible economic policies, economic growth is likely to be rapid, which will in turn contribute to continued political stability. Economic growth alone may not be capable of damping the tensions that could upset the political system, but it is hard to imagine how these tensions can be kept under control in the *absence* of sustained economic growth.

IV. Scenario One: The high growth alternative

If one accepts the broad outline of the arguments presented above, it is possible to put together alternative scenarios of how the Chinese economy might evolve over the next two decades. The first scenario assumes that China will continue to grow at a rate of 8 or 9 per cent per year, much like it has for the past seventeen years. For this scenario to be realised, most things – although not everything – will have to go right for China, both internally and externally.

The external requirements for high growth are the most straightforward. World markets must remain open to expanding Chinese exports. There is no need for those exports to expand at the rate of the past decade, but they do need to grow as fast as the Chinese economy as a whole, or a bit faster. With real export growth rates of 8 to 11 per cent a year, China will have the foreign exchange it needs to break most economic bottlenecks, and large sections of Chinese industry will be under constant pressure to meet international quality and cost standards. Foreign direct investment will also have to continue at a fairly high level. China has alternatives to FDI for earning foreign exchange and financing investment, but it needs the access to foreign markets, management skills and technology that sometimes only comes accompanied by FDI. The transition in Hong Kong in 1997, among other things, will have to go reasonably smoothly if these export or FDI objectives are to be realised.

The internal economic requirements for high growth are more complex. At the level of growth fundamentals, China will have to maintain a high rate of personal and corporate savings since the government is not likely again to be the major source of savings and investment. The quality of Chinese universities and research establishments will have to continue to be steadily expanded and upgraded. More will probably need to be done along these lines to get the best-trained Chinese now abroad to return home, although rising economic opportunity and a more open society may bring this about without additional special effort.

Continuing the reforms in the economic system will also be essential, but there is to date only a partial consensus as to which reforms really matter. It is generally agreed that the state-owned enterprises clearly cannot continue as they are. The accounting systems of these enterprises must be modernised and standardized so that it is possible to tell whether they are profitable or not. The tax authorities need to obey their own tax laws and stop acting like nineteenth century Chinese officials who treated any local enterprise as a cash cow. The social welfare system must be separated from the enterprise through the creation of national systems, whether public or private. Perhaps most difficult of all, enterprise management needs to be selected by independent profit-oriented boards of directors rather than by government ministries or the State Council.

If the state enterprises can be transferred, the banks and other components of the financial system can also be reformed and brought up to the standards required by a market economy. It is unrealistic to expect the government to allow the large state-owned banks to go bankrupt. However, at the very least, political criteria need to be removed from bank lending, and bank management must be made to pay a price (firing or demotion) when the bank is mismanaged. The separation of the commercial banks from policy lending is a start in the right direction, but only a start.

If the state-owned enterprises can be reformed, then controlling inflation should not be difficult. Most inflationary pressure in China is generated by excessive lending to state enterprises that frequently do not repay their loans. Regularising the tax system, something needed for state enterprise reform, will also help keep the government's budget deficit under control. Cost push factors, for the most part, are not a major source of inflation in China. The large surplus of labour, for example, ensures that wage agreements are not a source of inflationary pressure.

Controlling corruption presents a bigger challenge. The high growth scenario assumes that corruption will not spiral upwards to a point where the stability and credibility of the Chinese government is undermined. Anti-corruption campaigns, no matter how many people are jailed or executed, will not do the job. The only solution is steady dismantlement of the controls and licences that provide opportunities for rent-seeking. A transparent, well-functioning land market would also be a help.

If all of the reforms described above are carried out, then high growth itself should damp down the other major potential source of political instability, the floating population of surplus workers. Urban, township and village jobs will continue to grow rapidly, and most who seek employment will receive some degree of satisfaction.

If most of the population is preoccupied with becoming "rich", it may not matter that much to the economy whether the top leadership of the government and the Party is united and stable. The name of the person or people in charge of the government will make a difference for particular projects and particular policy decisions, but will not have much influence on the environment for most foreign and domestic investments.

V. Scenario Two: A deteriorating external environment

A deteriorating external environment for China's economy could come about in several ways. The most straightforward, and the one most probable, would be for China's own rapid export growth to trigger a protectionist reaction in its major foreign markets. Such a reaction is most likely if China is widely perceived as keeping its own market relatively closed and if it runs a large balance-of-trade surplus with the world on a sustained basis. Even bilateral trade surpluses can be a problem, as current economic relations between China and the United States demonstrate, but there is less China can do about bilateral imbalances. The country cannot throw its overall balance of payments into a sustained deficit in order to solve a bilateral imbalance.

A mishandling of the Hong Kong transition, if China were widely perceived to be at fault, might also trigger a protectionist reaction, as might various scenarios of what could happen in the Straits of Taiwan or the South China Sea. More generally, China's overall foreign policy posture, or the way the major powers perceive that posture, will have an influence on whether those powers and their allies keep their markets open to China. These same external forces also could trigger perceptions among potential foreign investors in China that the country is too risky an environment for FDI.

If protectionist forces do become predominant *vis-à-vis* China, then the scenario of high export growth projections will no longer be feasible. The export-to-GNP ratio could actually begin to fall, in which case China would become increasingly dependent on its own domestic market. What would happen to overall economic growth if this were to occur?

At a theoretical level, it is not difficult to construct a story about how declining involvement in foreign trade would lead industry to reorient itself smoothly toward the domestic market. There would be fewer imports embodying the latest technology, but the government and industry could turn to other ways of gaining access to the best techniques. However, this outcome implies that China could turn inward while simultaneously moving toward a highly flexible, fully reformed market economy and an open society that, among other things, would draw tens of thousands of Chinese research scientists back home from overseas. Such an outcome is not very realistic.

More realistic is an outcome where tensions connected with turning inward reinforce the political position of those who were suspicious of the turn outward in the first place. This view is most often associated with a general suspicion of market forces and a preference for planning and an active government role. The number of government licences and approvals required per project would increase rather than decrease. Independent boards of directors with the power to appoint managers would be anathema. Control and selection of management would rest squarely in the government and the Party.

The direct impact of these changes would be to halt the market reform process in its tracks. There would be no backtracking to outright central planning and a Soviet-style command system, but bureaucratic interventions in the economy would be pervasive. China's economic system might look much like that of Hungary's in the 1980s. More interventions would mean more corruption. Unreformed state enterprises would be a source of periodic bursts of inflationary pressure, as in the past.

The combination of slow export growth and an urban economic system with pervasive government controls would slow growth by at least two or three percentage points a year. Slower growth would mean fewer employment opportunities, which would increase social tension. Tension among the underemployed could reinforce discontent caused by high levels of corruption and periodic bouts of inflation. The resulting instability in the political system would probably reduce growth even further, which would increase tensions – and a downward spiral would be under way.

32

Barring an outright collapse of the political system, however, growth in the economy will not come to a halt. During the two decades that contained the disastrous economic policies of the Great Leap Forward and the Cultural Revolution (1957-78), China still managed an average GNP growth rate of 4.5 per cent per year. This scenario thus has China looking more and more like the Soviet Union of the 1970s and 1980s. Confrontational international relations would be combined with substantial internal social and political tensions. The economy would continue to grow and technology would improve, but China's more limited capacities might be focused increasingly on maintaining and strengthening the military.

VI. Scenario Three: The triumph of the bureaucracy

Even if the external environment remains open to growing Chinese exports, foreign direct investment, and technology transfers, China might not escape many of the problems outlined in Scenario Two. Internal forces could produce some, but not all, of the same outcomes.

China's government bureaucracy is clearly reluctant to let go of the levers of power, much like bureaucracies elsewhere in the world. That reluctance often has been overcome during the reform period by the willingness of Party leaders to override these interests, even though that meant a diminution in the power of the Party itself. These leaders could take that risk because, with Deng Xiaoping in charge, the political system was quite secure.

But what will happen if a future weakened leadership depends on the government bureaucracy as a pillar of its political support? And what will happen if that same leadership sees the levers of bureaucratic control as essential to keeping political control over parts of the population? Then, the interests of the political leadership and the government bureaucracy will merge.

The most obvious result of this merger of interests will be the initial triumph of the bureaucratic approach to economic development. Investment decisions of any scale will remain in the hands of Beijing or of provincial capitals. Licensing will be pervasive. Enterprises will be merged into large conglomerates which will be said to be patterned after the Korean *chaebol* or Japanese *keiretsu*. In reality, these conglomerates will be more like old ministries or bureaus, with only the veneer of true autonomy. Price controls will be a common if futile means of controlling inflation. Bank credit will remain subject to political influence.

The immediate impact of this triumph of bureaucratic interests would much resemble what would happen under Scenario Two. Corruption would be pervasive and there would be periodic bouts of inflation. Growth would be slower and the underemployed would have difficulty finding good jobs, further fueling discontent. This discontent would strengthen the leadership's feelings of insecurity, reinforcing its desire to hold onto the levers of bureaucratic control.

If the external economic environment proves open and supportive, the downward spiral of Scenario Two would be less likely. Powerful offsetting forces would limit and ultimately undermine the triumph of bureaucratic intervention. The most powerful of these forces would be the self-interest of those making the day-to-day economic decisions in enterprises. The township and village enterprises would be pressing the system to remove bureaucratic obstacles to higher profits and would be circumventing the obstacles that existed. The state-owned enterprise managers would themselves be fighting for autonomy as the only way of making their enterprises profitable and keeping their workers happy. Those managers who fail to see their interests in this way would increasingly be seen, even by their bureaucratic masters, as problems or failures.

These domestic market-oriented interests would have powerful external allies. Foreign markets and governments will insist on rules and performance criteria that can only be met under a market system. China's exports will grow, but only if China abides by international rules and its producers are highly sensitive to foreign market conditions. Foreign investors will continue to pour money into the country only if the foreign exchange market and the domestic market for goods and services become increasingly open. Many of the changes effected in the name of promoting foreign investment will in fact be mainly of benefit to domestic investors, freeing them up from unnecessary controls.

In this scenario, therefore, growth is not likely to slow as much as in the case where the external environment is hostile. Security concerns will not be a justification for further clamping down on the economy and on politics. Growth would thus fall below the high growth of Scenario One, but would be higher than the 4.5 per cent per year of Scenario Two.

VII. Conclusion

In the most realistic scenarios, the Chinese economy will continue to expand from its already substantial base. However, over a ten- or twenty-year period, the difference between 4.5 and 9 per cent per year in the growth of GNP is enormous.

For the people of China, the difference between these growth rates, which in per capita terms convert to 3 to 7.5 per cent per year, means a standard of living increase over twenty years of between 81 and 324 per cent. The former figure makes China's population better off, but a large share would still be struggling to get along on minuscule plots of land. Those in non-agricultural employment would be doing better, but they would be living in a China that continued to be engulfed by political tension and periodic disruptions of varying magnitudes. Much of the increase in GNP might end up diverted toward the military or to other areas of waste and inefficiency. At the higher growth figure, China could become an urban, increasingly "middle class" society with a standard of living not far below that of South Korea today.

For the outside world, the contrast in outcomes is equally stark. There are few benefits for the international economy in the slow growth scenarios. China's demand for grain imports will not increase much because incomes will be growing only slowly and that will keep prices for other grain importers (and exporters) lower, which could perhaps be considered a benefit. Industrial emissions that pollute the environment may not be all that different under any of the scenarios. Slower growth might mean slower increases in energy use and hence in CO_2 emissions, but slower growth is also likely to be accompanied by fewer reforms that promote the efficient use of energy and alternative energy sources to coal. Fast growth built on the increasingly efficient use of energy and changes away from coal might not produce all that much more CO_2.

Chinese military expenditures might also grow more slowly if GNP is only increasing by 4.5 per cent per year, but not necessarily that much more slowly. A China racked by tensions at home and in a confrontational relationship with the outside world will find ways to channel increasing funds to the military. A rapidly growing China will find it easier to raise military expenditures, but will be under far less pressure actually to do so.

Which of the three scenarios – if not some fourth alternative – will be realised? The answer will depend mostly on internal forces within China. However, as this essay has argued, China's external environment will also play an important part in determining which of these internal forces ends up dominating the future.

Notes

1. The 4.5 per cent figure is lower than the official growth rate figure for the 1957-78 period. It was estimated by revaluing Chinese GDP at 1980 prices rather than earlier-year prices that inflate the contribution of industry to GDP growth. China's official GDP figures for 1979-95 generate a growth rate slightly above 9 per cent, but Chinese national accounts procedures are widely believed to overstate real GDP growth by an unknown (if probably small) amount.

2. The Chinese and Soviet concept of net material product (or, in their terminology, national income) is equivalent to GDP minus certain services. The concept of accumulation differs from gross domestic capital formation in a similar way, but the percentages obtained using GDCF/GDP are not likely to differ much from accumulation/NMP percentages.

3. China has not joined the UN system for calculating purchasing power parity exchange rates, and so all that is available is the work of outsiders using less complete sets of data. These estimates are updated versions of the low estimates made by Ruoen and Kai, 1995; see also Keidel, 1994.

Bibliography

KEIDEL, Albert (1994), *China: GNP per Capita,* World Bank, Washington, DC, December.

RUOEN, Ren and Chen KAI (1995), "An Expenditure-Based Bilateral Comparison of Gross Domestic Product between China and the United States", World Bank, Policy Research Working Paper No. 1415, January.

The Outlook for Labour-intensive Manufacturing in China

by

Vincent Cable
Chief Economist, Shell International

I. Slippery concepts

A number of important questions arise in defining the subject of this chapter. While the concept of "labour-intensive, low-wage, low-tech" manufacturers is in widespread popular usage, it is often not at all clear what it means. Industries such as garment manufacturing are generally assumed to be "labour-intensive" on account of specific processes (sewing, cutting embroidery), but some of these have yielded to whole or partial automation; they may well have a capital-intensive and technologically sophisticated internal infrastructure (the inventory management and delivery system of a Benetton); and a wider definition might change their character (textile-spinning and, to a lesser extent, weaving are very capital-intensive even if "downstream" finishing is not). Some capital- and knowledge-intensive "information" industries may well have segments which involve labour-intensive assembly (of PCs, for example) or skilled labour- but not capital-intensive activities (some aspects of computer programming). The same product can be made using totally different technologies (textile weaving from the most sophisticated, high-speed machines to the hand loom).

The analysis is further complicated by the distorted character of the Chinese economy. A "labour-intensive" Chinese state-owned steel complex using 1950s/60s Russian technology and heavily buttressed by subsidy may employ many times the labour force of a "capital-intensive" Western, Japanese or Korean plant manufacturing the same tonnage, and may employ more labour in relation to capital utilised – capital is itself an ambiguous concept in China – than a Chinese light manufacturing plant outside the state sector. Vintages of technology, ownership and location may therefore be far more significant determinants of factor intensity than the product. In any event, the uneven quality of Chinese data makes analysis difficult.

So that the discussion does not get bogged down in definitional issues, "labour-intensive" is discussed here in very loose terms. Essentially, it covers industries that fall

37

within the SITC 8 sector, but it can also encompass some of SITC 7 (machinery) and SITC 6 (semi-processed items).

II. Labour-intensive manufacturing and economic reform

Several independent strands in Chinese policy have shaped labour-intensive manufacturing. The first is *enterprise reform* – in particular the encouragement of non-state, small-scale firms, especially township and village enterprises (TVEs). These had their origin in Mao's programmes of rural industrialisation, but after 1984 local governments were encouraged to develop them. Their share of gross industrial output rose from 10 per cent in 1980 to 45 per cent in 1993; also in the latter year, together with urban industrial "collectives" and fully private firms, they accounted for a majority (57 per cent) of industrial production.

When comparisons were last made (in the late 1980s), labour employed per unit of output by TVEs averaged around two and a half times that of state firms (and over twice that of "small" state firms), while private firms had five times the labour intensity of state firms (Jefferson and Rawski, 1994).

But total factor productivity (TFP) has been growing more rapidly – 4.5 per cent per annum in the 1980s as against 2 per cent for state enterprise – so that the level of TFP in "collectives" was higher than in state enterprise by the end of the 1980s, after having begun at the same level in 1980 (Jefferson, Rawski and Zheng, 1992).

Key elements that have produced a form of manufacturing enterprise that is efficient, rapidly growing and labour-intensive are several. There is a "hard" budget constraint, because local government cannot engage in deficit financing. Moreover, any surpluses accrue to local communities (and their leaders) so that they have a stake, in terms of both income and prestige, in the success of the enterprise. There is also intense competition in Chinese (and, increasingly, overseas) markets. Local – unlike national – government is not able to protect TVEs from competition, and rivalry between different areas for resources and foreign partners is a powerful stimulus. Because of competitive pressures, there is a corresponding motivation to depoliticise enterprises and to bring in professional management. Because there is no job security and (thus) none of the politically constrained approach to enterprise management associated with the "iron rice bowl" in state enterprises, firms can expand or contract their labour force as required, in a flexible labour market.

The lack of social overheads and labour regulation, and the ease of hire and fire, encourage labour-intensive production methods. The cost of labour is low and can be cut in adverse market conditions. Other forms of regulation are lightly applied, if at all. The upshot is that the collective aspect of ownership associated with TVEs is insignificant; in practice, they correspond closely to competitive, private firms.

The second relevant aspect of policy reform has been in *trade policy,* and related areas such as exchange rate determination and FDI policy. In 1978 China's trade was heavily influenced by central planning, which covered 100 per cent of exports; by 1992, however, that figure was only 15 per cent (Lardy, 1992; Fukasaku, Wall and Wu, 1994).

Planners' preferences corresponded only weakly and coincidentally with comparative advantage. Subsequently, the share of capital-intensive manufactures in total exports fell from 50 per cent in 1975 to 35 per cent in 1980 and then to under 20 per cent by 1990, while the share of labour-intensive manufactures rose from 36 per cent in 1975 and 39 per cent in 1980 to 74 per cent in 1990 (World Bank, 1993).

This change is the product of interrelated and evolving reforms of the trade policy regime (described in detail in Yuangshuo, forthcoming): the reduction of direct administrative control over trade; decentralisation of national foreign trade businesses (which then soared in number from 12 to several thousand); de-licensing; reduced protection of the home market through tariffication and tariff reduction; reduction of disincentives to exports (subsidies for high-priced imported inputs and tax rebates); an import regime which makes importing materials for processing in China attractive (47 per cent of China's exports in 1994); and a move to a market-determined, heavily devalued exchange rate in real effective terms, which is attractive to exporters (a devaluation of over 300 per cent in real terms since 1984).

The story is a complex one, and far from complete since there are still many distortions, but one survey concludes: "China has successfully converted its export structure to one that is increasingly determined by comparative advantage and has become a competitive exporter of manufactured goods in the world market'' (Fukasaku, Wall and Wu, 1994, p. 65).

Trade policy reform alone, however, cannot explain the shift of China's export structure to labour-intensive manufacturing. Enterprise reform is also involved. Township and village enterprises made a significant contribution to this transformation; their share of exports rose from 4 per cent in 1980 to a third in 1993. TVEs do not directly carry out foreign trade business but are flexible, and rapid to respond to changes in world market conditions mediated through the foreign trade companies (Byrd and Qingsong, 1990; Singh, Ratha and Nan, 1993). In addition, foreign investors contributed to the rise in exports from 3 per cent in 1987 to 27 per cent in 1993. The opening up of China to wholly owned foreign investment, especially in export-oriented projects, has introduced into the country intentionally mobile firms seeking to benefit from China's absolute (rather than comparative) advantage in low wage costs.

Another important element in the overall picture is the creation of Special Economic Zones, within which market reforms, foreign investment and exports have had exceptional support and the benefit of incentives (exports, for example, were freed from duties and indirect taxes).

The enormous growth and structural changes in China's exports have thus come from interlocking sets of reforms. Without freeing up prices, it would not have been possible to let go of mandatory export and import prices. Without enterprise reform, there would not have been the businesses to respond to trade policy incentives. Without FDI liberalisation, it could have been more difficult to attract investors with access to international marketing networks and the quality and technology that are necessary complements to low labour costs, especially in processing and assembly operations, for such items as machinery and electronic goods.

The third influence is changing *domestic demand,* and the influence reform has had on that demand. The overwhelming majority of labour-intensive manufacturing – notably by the TVEs – is intended for domestic rather than foreign markets, though there is no reliable benchmark for measuring the proportion. There is, in addition, no data readily available which would permit cross-comparisons between the structure of consumption and the production characteristics of Chinese industry. It can be said, however, that the encouragement given to light industry through reform has been designed to provide mass consumption products, while simultaneously generating employment in labour-intensive industries. In the period 1952-78, the output of heavy industry rose 40 times while that of light industry rose only 16 times. From 1978 to 1990, light industry grew more rapidly (14 per cent versus 10.5 per cent for heavy industry), though the trends seem to have shifted back again after 1990.

The development of light industry was facilitated by the removal of planning constraints and the creation of a domestic mass market for consumer goods accompanied by rapid economic growth and a freeing-up of the retail system. There have been high penetration levels in urban areas and the most prosperous rural districts for colour TVs, refrigerators, washing machines, furniture combinations, soft beds, fans and fashionable clothing – over and above the more established consumer products like bicycles, sewing machines, blankets, staple foods and cigarettes. While some of the rapidly expanding consumer durable markets are being serviced by capital-intensive production lines, most consumer products originate in labour-intensive production systems of the TVEs and similar enterprise types.

III. Future trends and forces

There are both direct and indirect influences on the development of labour-intensive manufacturing industry in China – some internal to China, some external. If, however, the combined influence is to propel China further towards being an open market economy, then there should be a commensurate expansion of labour-intensive manufacturing in domestic and foreign markets.

China has an enormous reservoir of labour with a very low opportunity cost, and a functioning market economy should support both an economically efficient use of relatively abundant resources and a pattern of new investment and technological change which also reflects relative factor availability. Within this broad framework, there are several more specific policy domains.

Domestic trade policy

Despite China's formidable performance in international trade, moving up from the 36th to the 10th market exporter internationally since 1978 and increasing its share of world trade from 0.9 to 2.8 per cent, China falls well short of having a non-discriminatory, market-based, transparent trade policy regime. It is under strong pressure to reform in that direction, both domestically and from China's partners, through conditions set for

Chinese admission to the World Trade Organisation. The so-called US "roadmap" now provides a realistic hope that China will be accommodated within multilateral rules and specific objectives for trade policy reform (not all of them liberal, *e.g.* "safeguards" for Western economies). Four main issues have yet to be resolved in the liberalisation of China's own trade regime.

State trading companies and trading rights

There are still substantial restrictions on the freedom of enterprises to engage in both export and import on their own account – a freedom reserved mainly for state trading corporations and large state enterprises. As an OECD Development Centre study notes, "the decentralisation of the *process* of trading does not mean that trade was becoming market-determined in the same proportion. Trade in products covered by mandatory plans was still highly centralised and that covered by guidance plans still subject to tight controls... Permission to import was still rigidly controlled by licensing, and export procurement was still carried out in the price 'airlock' and still subject to government control of resource allocation in factor and intermediate goods markets" (Fukasaku, Wall and Wu, 1994, p. 28). The process of rationalising trade structure according to market-determined comparative advantage is by no means complete.

Non-tariff business and tariff levels

Despite a shift to tariffs – a more transparent system of protection – there remains extensive licensing for a mixture of protectionist and balance-of-payments reasons. (The existing proportions of tariffs and licensing are unclear, and a bone of contention in the WTO negotiation.) There does seem to be a bias towards the protection of finished consumer durable goods (*e.g.* colour TVs, cars, refrigerators), both by excluding imports and by exempting components from controls.

The same bias (and exceptions) exist for tariffs, which – with an average unweighted nominal protection rate of around 35 per cent (consumer goods 65 per cent) – are high by the standards of any country except, perhaps, India (Pritchett and Sethi, 1994). Although most highly protected industries employ mature technology, the effect of supporting them artificially is probably to encourage relatively capital-intensive production methods, using tariff- and quota-exempt imported equipment. Liberalisation should have the opposite effect, which indeed seems to be occurring as tariff exceptions are being removed and levels reduced. The Chinese Government has undertaken to reduce the tariff level to an average of 15 per cent.

Subsidies

Agricultural exporters are in part supported by subsidy, and many of the state-owned industries are able to produce (and export) only with the help of subsidies. Greater transparency and discipline are being sought, which – again – will favour those exports and import-competing activities that are genuinely competitive in a market environment, such as the labour-intensive products of TVEs.

41

Implementation

Many of the difficulties of negotiating with China centre on the gap between formal government positions and reality on the ground. The continued frustrations over intellectual property rights relate to weak or non-existent implementation of agreements at provincial level. The complexities of the standards and products inspection system and the endless procedural problems encountered by foreign investors are sometimes interpreted as proof of a deep mercantilist commitment. More plausibly, they are the inevitable but temporary frictions of a system evolving from state-directed, autarkic development to openness and market orientation within a generation.

Overall, a quick resolution of the terms of China's admission to the WTO (which encompasses other issues such as national treatment in the services sector for foreign investors), and in particular an early phasing in of trade policy liberalisation commitments, could hasten market-based restructuring. How precisely this would play out is difficult to predict. While Chinese import-substituting, consumer goods manufacturing has been exposed to some competition from inward investors and from smuggled goods, freer availability of goods might change production structure and techniques of production in unexpected ways.

Trade policy overseas

A key constraint on the future expansion of labour-intensive manufactured exports is trade policy in the main Western markets – although in the long term the opening up of Asian markets, as a result of the APEC and AFTA processes, could prove more important. At present there are several impediments. One is that, in general, labour-intensive manufactured products face relatively high access barriers in OECD markets, reflected both in tariff levels and in the incidence of NTBs. Almost a quarter of China's exports are covered by textile and garment quotas (though there is a good deal of Hong Kong re-export trade in this sector). UNCTAD figures suggest that 60 per cent of China's manufactured exports to the United States faced trade barriers (28 per cent for all LDCs), as did 40 per cent of its exports to the European Union (32 per cent for all LDCs).

A second problem is that as a non-member of the GATT/WTO, China does not enjoy most favoured nation status as a right and faces either a politically bruising annual renewal of MFN status (in the United States) or discriminatory treatment elsewhere.

Third, the lack of transparency in the pricing of China's state enterprises and STCs has laid them open to anti-dumping action (even though the motive may be quite different: a reaction to Chinese competitiveness). China is, according to the latest WTO figures, by far the largest victim of anti-dumping actions at present.

Despite periodic worries about growing protectionism in the West, the "worst case" fears have so far proved largely groundless. The Uruguay Round was completed. The textiles MFA, of particular concern to China (though technically its quotas, like those of Chinese Taipei, are not MFA restrictions), is being phased out, albeit slowly. Also, most favoured nation negotiations have completed passage through the US Congress, despite concerns over human rights. The mere fact that China's exports have grown so prodigiously does not suggest that there is the will, even if there were the wish, to stop rapid Chinese export expansion.

Even if the WTO accession proceeds smoothly, however, and there is no serious deterioration in the overall global trade policy environment, there are still considerable potential barriers that could face Chinese manufactured exports. The European Union is insisting on maintaining selective safeguards and "anti-surge" mechanisms for Chinese products, and the United States will not surrender regular MFN review. Trade barriers have started to appear against Chinese exports to Japan.

There are also perhaps deeper problems ahead. China will face growing competition from India, which has a similar endowment of limitless supplies of low-cost labour and substantial availability of highly skilled and educated manpower. China's revealed comparative advantage is highly correlated with that of India (and South East Asian countries) for machinery and miscellaneous manufactures (author's estimates). After 1997, China's exports will include those of Hong Kong, which may in the past have benefited from its distinctively open and free trading traditions but could in future suffer from whatever adverse political or protectionist sentiment is directed at the People's Republic of China.

Hitherto, China has had rapid export growth from a very low base. In the future the same percentage increase translates into larger absolute volumes, and those sectional interests which see themselves as threatened by Chinese competition will be correspondingly more vociferous. China already accounts for over 5 per cent of OECD imports in some significant product areas (travel goods, clothing, furniture, textiles, telecoms and recording equipment, miscellaneous manufactures) and its presence in the market is becoming highly visible and a target for pressure groups seeking to restrict trade. On the other hand, its exports are among the most diverse of any country (author's calculations of Hirschman index).

One of the main values of the WTO accession in this context is that Western governments may find it easier to resist populist agitation against Chinese "cheap labour" when operating within the discipline of multilateral rules.

Exchange rates

One of the main stimuli for export expansion has been the depreciation of the *renminbi* – in real as well as nominal terms. The ratio of exports to GDP has risen from 5 per cent in 1978 to 9.5 per cent in 1985 to 23 per cent in 1994 as real exchange rate depreciation has provided a powerful incentive to the production of tradeables, and exports in particular.

Long-term exchange rate prediction is a notoriously unsatisfactory exercise, since there are quite different views about what causes exchange rates to move. From a current account balance-of-payments equilibrium standpoint, the exchange rate does not look seriously out of line. There is currently (1994 data) a small trade surplus (about $5 billion, or 1 per cent of nominal GDP in 1994) after years of both surpluses and deficits (with a cumulative net deficit since 1978 of around $30 billion, and deficits in eleven of the seventeen years since 1978). Trade policy liberalisation should increase net imports in the short run and, other things being equal, bring downward pressure on the exchange rate. An offsetting factor is that there are very high levels of reserves, currently over $70 billion, which could absorb some of the shock of import liberalisation.

However, there is a radically different interpretation suggested by the purchasing power parity value of the Chinese currency: that it is enormously undervalued in relation to the dollar (and by extension to other leading currencies). Meaningful comparisons of prices between China and the main OECD countries are very difficult but suggest that on a purchasing power parity basis, China's average per capita income is far higher than the $470 (in 1992) suggested by conventional conversions of the domestic currency GDP per head at the current market exchange rate: as high as $3 000, with even very conservative estimates (such as Lardy's) at $1 000 to $1 200 (for further discussion see Lardy, 1994 and Cable, 1995).

These figures have hitherto created excitement largely because of what they imply about the true size of China's domestic market (and because they suggest that China's aid worthiness as a low-income country may not be as compelling as originally thought). But there are radical implications for future exchange rate movements. One is that the exchange rate will, in the future, appreciate strongly in real terms. This could occur through nominal appreciation – as has occurred with other East Asian currencies, notably the yen and, more recently, the won – or, more probably, through relatively high inflation.

The prices of traded goods and services in a competitive market economy will be constrained by world prices, but the nontraded segments of the economy (by far the largest) could experience inflation, raising prices to international levels. This could in turn make Chinese nontradeable production – especially services – more profitable than internationally traded production and attract resources out of the traded goods sector. Under these circumstances, there would be a strong disincentive to maintain export growth at past rates.

The important implication is counter-intuitive: that a more open, market-oriented China could also become more inward-looking, with relatively high growth in sectors serving the home market. This is not perhaps as surprising as it may seem. Other "big" open economies only export a small part of their GNP – just over 10 per cent in the case of the United States. There are strong advantages, such as economies of scale, from the domestic market. The process of becoming a "normal" economy with a strong home market may be a very difficult one for China – there is a poor internal transport infrastructure, for example – but the main conclusion for labour-intensive manufacturing is that there is unlikely to be a lasting strong incentive to export from a weak currency. Whether this adjustment takes place over five years or fifty is obviously crucial.

IV. Labour markets

The explanation usually given for China's economically efficient use of relatively labour-intensive production methods – and its bias in trade towards labour-intensive manufacturing – is that labour in China is abundant, and cheap.

While that is indeed generally the case, China is still very far from having a "free" labour market. There are impediments to mobility presented by "household registration": in effect, a system of internal passports. That system does now seem to be breaking down, overwhelmed by large numbers of immigrants from the interior to the more prosperous and rapidly growing provinces. But there is also the "danwei" system, another major impediment, which provides both job security and welfare, and close control over urban workers, mainly in state-owned enterprises.

There are at least 50 million workers directly employed in state-owned enterprises (SOEs), of which 15 million may be redundant but still drawing pay and entitlements. At least a third of the 11 000 large and medium-sized enterprises are losing money and another third are on the margins of viability, largely because the authorities fear the consequences of labour retrenchment.

The wider consequences for the economy of this drain on resources have been widely discussed: the inflationary effects of central government deficits swollen by SOE losses; contamination of the banking system, with bad debt deriving from forced lending to the SOEs; the diversion of scarce capital investment into low-productivity investment by SOEs – an estimated 60 per cent of total fixed investment as against 23 per cent of GDP accounted for by SOEs; investment feasts and famine that have aggravated the inflationary stop-go cycle.

A freeing up of the Chinese labour market and, in particular, the shedding of large numbers of workers from restructuring state enterprises will have implications for labour-intensive manufacturing in both TVEs and FDI enterprises. These enterprises will become more important as they absorb unemployed labour, and should find it easier to expand since credit and materials, hitherto pre-empted by state enterprises, will be more easily available. The government is currently funding "employment service enterprises" with cheap loans to absorb the unemployed (it is claimed that 10 million are working in such enterprises; many would appear to be TVEs).

If China becomes a "free" labour market, there will be a large overhang of surplus workers to absorb: an estimated 130 million from the countryside, plus whatever number is released by a contracting state enterprise sector. The establishment of a social security system for urban workers in Hainan (and elsewhere) establishes, in effect, a reservation wage in a more flexible labour market as SOEs contract; however, that wage could easily be overwhelmed by inter-regional and rural-urban migration.

In these circumstances, it should be easy for Chinese and foreign employers in urban and rural areas to acquire labour cheaply or on flexible conditions of employment (that is, with limited job security and other worker protection). The poor conditions and insecurity associated with work in the TVEs could become more widespread.

In practice, the position is much more complex. Despite authoritarian government, there are many reports from China of labour unrest as workers organise, sometimes violently, to resist low pay and deteriorating conditions, particularly poor safety. The experience of countries with a more pluralistic tradition, such as India, does not suggest that the availability of vast labour surpluses translates at all smoothly into a cheap, docile and efficient workforce. There are, moreover, costs – possibly substantial – in training, accommodating and motivating unskilled workers with a rural background to become productive employees. These important qualifications notwithstanding, the overall impact of freeing up labour markets in China, including the effect of removing subsidies from SOEs, will be to give a substantial impetus to labour-intensive manufacturing for domestic and foreign markets.

There are two other major imponderables as regards the development of the labour market. The rapid growth of the Chinese economy has been skewed towards the coastal provinces, overwhelmingly so where export activities are concerned. Real wages are reported to have increased in certain areas following the earlier pattern developed in the NICs – Korea, Chinese Taipei, Singapore, Hong Kong – as rapid development of labour-intensive manufacturing began to exhaust easily available labour supplies. One of two things can now happen (assuming that market forces are allowed to operate). One is a migration of labour-intensive manufacturing further inland, although this is constrained by poor road and rail infrastructure for transporting inputs to the plants and output to domestic and foreign markets. The other is labour migration to the coastal areas, which will begin to create housing and social strains within the receiving areas. In practice, both processes are happening and will probably spread.

A second question is the availability of educated and skilled manpower. This is less of a problem for labour-intensive manufacturing in traditional industries than in high-tech activities; nevertheless, good management, marketing skills, supervisors, accountants and engineers among others will enjoy a market premium, particularly where international competition is involved.

V. FDI

Inward foreign investment has been very important at the margin in stimulating Chinese exports of labour-intensive manufacturing. The contribution of foreign investment to exports grew from 3 per cent in 1987 to 27.5 per cent in 1993. Much of this investment was from the Chinese diaspora in Hong Kong, Chinese Taipei and elsewhere subcontracting labour-intensive operations to China, particularly to the Special Economic Zones where fiscal inducements are available. (There is also a large but unquantifiable amount of FDI from offshore Chinese operations completing a ''round trip'' of foreign exchange control and tax evasion.) A modest amount of the FDI is by foreign multinationals using China as a cost-efficient location for labour-intensive manufacturing. However, the motivation for much FDI is to service the Chinese market and involves production facilities which are not, in Chinese terms, labour-intensive.

In the short term, at least, it seems highly unlikely that many Western (or Japanese) companies will conduct much labour-intensive manufacturing in China as part of their global operations. China is acquiring a reputation as a difficult country in which to invest: a large proportion of investors are losing money; the transport system is poor for both internal and external distribution; the legal system is often seen as alien and biased; corruption is on an epic scale – in league tables complied by businessmen, China is close to the top along with Indonesia, India, Russia and Nigeria; and there is little transparency in rules and procedures. There has been a growing awareness among economists of the ideas associated with Douglas North – among others, that systems of law and trust in public institutions count heavily in creating an efficient, sustainable form of capitalism. For many foreign investors, China so far fails that test. Over time, however, confidence will grow and encourage multinationals to use China as part of their production systems.

The view of the Chinese diaspora is somewhat different, since it has advantages of language, connections and familiarity with local investors. A great deal of FDI has already come from this source. It is possible that mainland China will become the focal point of the Hua Ch'iao – the network or commonwealth of overseas Chinese. To a degree this is already happening: through assimilation (Hong Kong), conscious strategy (Singapore) or by turning a blind political eye to commercial realities (Chinese Taipei). But overseas Chinese investors also share many of the anxieties about China of Western and Japanese counterparts, and thus their role is almost certainly complementary to, rather than a substitute for, other FDI flows.

To some degree there is a conflict between the objectives of attracting FDI and moving towards a non-discriminatory market economy. The Chinese Government has begun to phase out some special inducements: tariff exceptions for foreign companies importing equipment and value-added rebates on exports. There is also a compelling argument that while Chinese Special Economic Zones played a very important part in allowing experiments for opening up the Chinese economy, the special inducements for Chinese and foreign investors (tax breaks, duty free exports, freedom from planning controls) are a source of economic inefficiency – not to mention fraud – and should be phased out, allowing the whole of China to enjoy market-friendly policies (Wall, 1993).

The connection between FDI – should it flow in growing volumes – and industrial structure is not at all clear. Different forms of FDI are driven by different motives: resource-based; domestic market-seeking; and export-oriented. Only the export-oriented component seems directly linked to labour-intensive manufacturing – but even here, the implications are unclear. Export-oriented FDI flows are determined by where China sits comparatively in terms of international absolute cost differences (weighted by political risk, among other factors). It is possible that China will evolve into a base for subcontracting labour-intensive parts of high-tech operations (like a McDonnell Douglas aircraft parts project) rather than a centre for more traditional labour-intensive industries. Anecdotes suggest that (as in India) foreign investors are more attracted by the potential for more sophisticated operations than simply the prospect of mobilising unskilled labour.

VI. Scenarios for the future

China could evolve in radically different ways, but the underlying demographic and labour force characteristics will not change. Whatever happens, there are 20 to 30 million new entrants to the labour market every year (though labour force growth is slowing); in addition, there are roughly 130 million persons living in rural areas who are not productively employed, with little prospect of expanding the available arable land. Although China has large numbers of highly educated and trained people in absolute terms, and is investing an exceptionally high proportion of GDP, it has, and will retain, a relative abundance of labour relative to capital, human or physical. A China in which resources are efficiently used will emphasize labour-intensive manufacturing (as well as services and agriculture) for foreign trade and production for domestic consumption.

Within that broad framework, several things could change on the political and economic front; this is what the scenarios below are designed to capture.

Scenario A

In one somewhat idealised story, China evolves much in the direction desired by its own economic reformers and Western trade partners and industries. Its open economy reforms would continue: ongoing trade liberalisation; the development of open and competitive markets for labour, capital, and capital and intermediate goods; clarification and transparency in FDI regulations; clearly defined property rights both for foreigners (intellectual property rights) and Chinese (*e.g.* TVEs); a continued move to currency convertibility; the ending of discriminatory arrangements such as the SEZs; reform leading to reduced subsidies for SOEs and state banking; and all within a framework of greater macroeconomic discipline. Since there is no precedent for a country of China's size achieving the kind of transformation described (except in China itself since 1978), there is no way of knowing what a transformed China would look like, or what problems would arise along the way. But this is probably a high (8 to 10 per cent)-growth scenario, albeit with considerable volatility as the reformers struggle to manage monetary and fiscal policy (and face new worries like the balance of payments).

What would such a scenario imply for labour-intensive manufacturing? First, trade policy reform should steer China's patterns of international specialisation even further in the direction of its comparative advantage. Exports of labour-intensive manufactures should continue to grow strongly, though exports will not indefinitely grow faster than Chinese GDP (and may grow more slowly with some real appreciation of the currency in the long term).

The question might be asked as to whether this growth will raise problems of absorptive capacity for OECD markets. Developing countries currently supply 3 to 4 per cent of all manufactured goods consumed in OECD Member countries, and China (excluding Hong Kong) around half of 1 per cent. If Member countries were to continue to grow at the same rate as in the 1980s and China's exports of manufactures were to continue to grow at around 15 per cent, then China's market share would reach 1 per cent by 2001, although obviously with much higher penetration in some markets. This is rather a small number (though growing), and should not present insurmountable problems provided trade with China continues to be defended politically as mutually beneficial. This case is easier to make if China is seen to be liberalising access for imports (and foreign investment). The rapid expansion and opening up of Asian markets to Chinese products would also take some of the political heat off the United States. One danger is that labour conditions in exporting firms in China may deteriorate with a freeing up of the labour market and more migration from the interior; that could in turn attract more of the attention of human rights activists, as well as protectionists armed with old but potent prejudices about cheap labour. Thus a favourable evolution of this scenario – as it applies to trade – assumes basic economic rationality in China and among China's trade partners.

Secondly, as confidence grows in China as a host for FDI, the country will be drawn into wider and deeper forms of collaboration with Western and Japanese companies; these will go beyond mere presence in the Chinese market and include specialised production facilities as part of wider corporate networks. Some obvious examples include vehicles and aircraft assembly, patented drugs and microchip manufacture. High-tech industries would not necessarily require high-tech operations in China; instead, production may involve a combination of local R&D work and labour-intensive assembly.

Thirdly, the process of public enterprise reform and the exposure of SOEs and the new firms of collective enterprise to international competition (through imports and FDI) will lead to sharper management and a clearer definition of ownership rights and responsibilities. What will emerge will be more efficient enterprises – perhaps, in the process, less labour-intensive ones – and some internationally competitive enterprises, which may well include a miscellany of metals manufacturing and engineering companies. Whether or not they are labour-intensive (taking into account their various upstream and downstream linkages) is perhaps not meaningfully measurable – but, on balance, they are likely to be.

Some might argue that a scenario even approximating the above could not happen in China. It requires a coincidence of favourable external and internal developments. It also requires a political system that is sufficiently flexible and devolved to allow a large measure of freedom in the movement of goods, capital, people and ideas. Finally – and simultaneously – it requires sufficient central authority to develop much better physical infrastructure to sustain order and to enforce the law.

It is all too easy to see how the liberalisation process in this scenario could spin out of control (which is precisely what China's more conservative leaders fear), leading to a loss of central government authority to the provinces (loss of fiscal revenue also leading to loss of control over the budget and monetary aggregates); a fragmentation of China's internal market; and a general weakening of law and order. In such a world, China would acquire the form but not the substance or efficiency of a market economy. Labour-intensive manufacturing could still flourish in the coastal areas, fed by a limitless supply of labour from the interior moving into increasingly squalid coastal cities that more resemble Dhaka or Manila than the Shanghai or Xiamen of today. To be sure, such an economy could support a substantial volume of labour-intensive manufacturing, but that manufacturing is likely to be of an unsophisticated, low-value-added kind operating in an unstable environment.

Scenario B

China might take a quite different trajectory. This would reflect the concerns of some conservative elements in the Chinese leadership regarding volatility and what they see as the corrosive effect of unfettered capitalism and unrestrained growth. The country would have a nationalistic, or mercantilist, approach to trade and foreign investment. It would be dominated by security concerns. And there would be scant interest in such issues as economic efficiency and comparative advantage. While a return to the wilder excesses of Maoism is highly improbable, a more measured approach to liberalisation and globalisation – the "Birdcage" strategy of the late Chen Yun, for example – is very plausible. A protectionist or generally hostile OECD would encourage such attitudes.

In the interests of stability and security, such a policy orientation would consciously settle for a lower rate of growth. Six per cent might be seen as sustainable – still impressive by most standards. There would be vigorous attempts to promote import substitution of foodstuffs and energy, and more emphasis on building up China's own technology, acquiring foreign ideas and partners on a selective basis. There would be no urgency to join the WTO except on terms acceptable to China, but this would not matter greatly; the continuing lure of the large and growing China market would provide some countervailing bargaining power if Western countries discriminated against China. The country would be in good company (Russia, for example).

Labour-intensive manufacturing would have an important but different role. Export-oriented enclaves would earn the foreign exchange to buy a more limited range of imports. Conscious intervention to diversify exports towards more capital-intensive and higher-tech products, perhaps on the Korean model, could help to diffuse some of the resistance overseas to traditional Chinese manufacturing exports. The main role of labour-intensive manufacturing, in TVE-type units, would be to soak up surplus labour and to provide basic consumer goods – durables and non-durables – to the home market. Shielded from international and transnational corporation brand competition, such units may lack sophistication, but internal competition would provide an adequate stimulus to keep costs low. The existence of a strong central government in China would provide the will and resources for developing internal infrastructure, which would in turn enable the underdeveloped internal markets to be integrated into a fully national economy with attendant economies of scale. State enterprises are tackled less vigorously than in Scenario A, but a gradual process of subsidy attrition and consensual improvements in productivity could slowly achieve results.

While such a scenario would disappoint many reform-minded Chinese, it could reassure many others. Provided it was managed pragmatically, there is no obvious reason why it should not be sustainable.

VII. Conclusion

Labour-intensive manufacturing already accounts for a large majority – over 80 per cent – of China's exports, and a substantial share of the 40 per cent of GDP contributed by manufacturing. Further reform in the direction of an open market economy should further increase these proportions of a rapidly growing total.

There are, however, some major imponderables. Chinese trade policy and the trade policies of OECD (and other) countries are obviously important. So is the regime for FDI and the functioning of collective enterprise, which accounts for much of labour-intensive manufacture. Less widely discussed but crucially important uncertainties include the real exchange rate; there could, for example, be substantial appreciation in the future. Moreover, there is a basic uncertainty over which development strategy China will take. Market opening and liberalisation cannot simply be assumed.

Bibliography

BYRD, William A. and Lin QINGSONG (1990), *China's Rural Industry: Structure, Development and Reform,* World Bank.

CABLE, V. (1995), *China and India: Economic Reform and Global Integration,* Royal Institute of International Affairs, London.

FUKASAKU, K., D. WALL and M. WU (1994), *China's Long March to An Open Economy,* OECD Development Centre.

JEFFERSON, Gary H. and Thomas G. RAWSKI (1994), "Enterprise Reform in Chinese Industry", *Journal of Economic Perspectives,* Vol. 8, No. 2, Spring.

JEFFERSON, Gary H., Thomas G. RAWSKI and Yuxin ZHENG (1992), "Growth Efficiency and Convergence in China's State and Collective Industry", *Economic Development and Cultural Change.*

LARDY, N.R. (1992), *Foreign Trade and Economic Reform in China 1978-90,* Cambridge University Press, Cambridge.

LARDY, N. (1994), *China in the World Economy,* Institute for International Economics, Washington, DC.

PRITCHETT, L. and G. SETHI (1994), *China: Foreign Trade Reform,* World Bank Country Study, Washington, DC.

SINGH, I., D. RATHA and Geny Xiao NAN (1993), *Enterprises as the Engine of Growth,* World Bank Policy Research Dept., May.

WALL, D. (1993), "China's Economic Reform and Opening Up Process: The Special Economic Zones", *Development Policy Review,* September.

WORLD BANK (1993), *China: Foreign Trade Reform: Meeting the Challenge of the 1990's,* Washington, DC.

Xu YUANGSHUO (forthcoming), "Chinese Trade Reforms and their Impact on Industry", Royal Institute of International Affairs Discussion Paper, Chatham House, London.

The Comparative Advantage of China's Manufacturing in the Twenty-first Century

by

Masaru Yoshitomi
Vice Chairman, Long-Term Credit Bank of Japan Research Institute

Compared with today, what unique features will distinguish China's comparative advantage in the twenty-first century?

I. Introduction

There is general agreement that since economic reforms were introduced in 1979, China has developed its comparative advantage over a relatively broad base of labour-intensive manufacturing, as indeed have most East Asian economies (Garnaut and Huang, 1995; Lardy, 1992; Yeats, 1991).

Several questions arise, however. First, does the sheer size of the Chinese economy have a bearing on the structure of China's comparative advantage? Secondly, does China's recent exporting of more capital- and technology-intensive products (*e.g.* telecommunications equipment, chemicals) indicate an earlier development and faster upgrading of comparative advantage in relation to other Asian developing nations, especially in view of the country's low level of per capita income? Thirdly, considering the extreme regional diversity of resource endowments in China's enormous economy, could the concentrated economic development taking place in the coastal areas give rise to a more advanced comparative advantage while the basic export structure remains essentially labour-intensive? Lastly, in light of the considerable accumulated human and physical capital in some areas of China – and the high technology policies in specifically designated zones – how will China's potential for technology development differ from those of other Asian NIEs?

By addressing these four questions in turn in the following sections, this paper highlights possible differences in comparative advantage and technological development that will differentiate China in the future from other Asian developing countries. The final section draws conclusions and discusses the implications of China's development for OECD countries.

II. Trade implications of China's scale

"Standard" arguments

"Standard" arguments posit that China, because of its vast scale, may have three advantages over the Asian NIEs (Chinese Taipei, South Korea, Singapore and Hong Kong) and ASEAN-4 countries (Thailand, Malaysia, Indonesia and the Philippines): a relative abundance of natural resources; a potentially huge domestic market; and a seemingly unlimited supply of surplus labour (Lau, 1994).

As it has one of the biggest land areas, China is indeed endowed with significant reserves of many mineral and agricultural resources. Its coal reserves, for example, are among the world's largest. The country also benefits from a variety of other natural resources that can be utilised for military and high-tech products.

China's huge population implies an equally huge potential domestic demand, which would permit economies of scale even in the absence of export markets. With an annual demand for vehicles of, say, one million – accounting for only 0.3 per cent of the total number of families – China can potentially support several "scale-efficient" plants, assuming a vehicle manufacturing plant's minimum efficient scale of about 0.2 million units per year.

China's firms can enjoy economies of scale not just at plant level but also at industry level, when the productivity of a firm depends on the size of the industry to which the firm belongs. This advantage can derive from, for instance, the active flow of news and ideas between firms, better access to suppliers of intermediate goods, or a large specialised labour market. The effect is known as Marshallian external economies.

An almost unlimited supply of surplus labour implies that the Chinese economy as a whole may be free of strong upward pressure on labour costs over the very long term. Economic growth thus may not be constrained by the shortage of labour, as it has been in Asian NIEs in recent years.

Counter-arguments

However, the actual economic developments that have taken place in China since economic reforms were launched fifteen years ago cast some doubt on these three advantages.

First of all, despite its vast land area and rich natural resources, exports of both mineral- and agriculture-intensive commodities have substantially declined in proportion to China's total exports: the former from 17.0 to 4.7 per cent during the period 1978-93, and the latter from 36.1 to 9.2 per cent. Thus, the aggregate share of both natural resource commodities declined from more than half (53.1 per cent) to less than one-seventh (13.9 per cent) in fifteen years (Table 1).

Rather surprisingly, China is not particularly well endowed with agricultural land. Per capita arable land area is only 0.08 hectares per person, much lower than the world average (0.25), most European countries (in Germany the figure is 0.15 and in France 0.32) and, of course, the western hemisphere (United States, 0.74; Argentina, 0.76; and Mexico, 0.26). Even among Asian countries, China's arable land per capita is only larger than Japan's (0.03), comparable to Indonesia's (0.09) and the Philippines' (0.07), and much smaller than India's (0.20) or Thailand's (0.33). "Although China occupies about 7 per cent of the world arable land which is equipped with already high grain yields by international standards, it may not be able to feed about 22 per cent of the world population at high consumption standards" (Garnaut and Huang, 1995).

The export focus is thus not on natural resource commodities, but on capital-intensive and labour-intensive manufactured products. Both account for an increasing share of China's total exports; the former rose from 15.2 to 28.8 per cent between 1978 and 1993, and the latter from 31.1 to 56.8 per cent.

Table 1. **China's total exports and imports by groups of commodities: 1978, 1980, 1985, 1990 and 1993**

Percentage

	1978	1980	1985	1990	1993
Exports					
Agriculture-intensive	36.1	26.3	21.7	12.5	9.2
Capital-intensive	15.2	15.6	12.8	26.7	28.8
Labour-intensive	31.1	30.2	35.4	50.9	56.8
Textile and clothing[a]	19.8	20.8	27.0	37.8	40.0
Mineral-intensive	17.0	27.3	28.8	9.4	4.7
Imports					
Agriculture-intensive	29.0	33.8	10.8	16.3	10.7
Capital-intensive	59.0	52.8	73.3	60.5	72.1
Labour-intensive	4.2	8.1	9.7	16.0	12.7
Textile and clothing[a]	1.7	4.3	5.2	9.3	9.5
Mineral-intensive	7.0	4.2	5.1	5.1	6.5

a) Textile and clothing are part of labour-intensive products which include SITC 65 (textile yarn, fabric, etc.) and 84 (clothing).

Source: Song and Zhao, 1995. (Original sources are UN trade data, International Economic Databank, the Australian National University.)

III. Is China's trade structure more advanced than those of other Asian developing countries?

The analysis above leads to the second question – whether China has specialised more rapidly in exporting capital-intensive and sophisticated products than other Asian economies at a similar development stage. The question is a legitimate one because the share of capital-intensive products in China's total exports has, since the mid-1980s, risen more rapidly than that of labour-intensive products. In 1992, exports of telecommunications equipment accounted for 5.4 per cent of total exports, and those of electrical equipment 2.3 per cent. Office machines, electrical machinery, watches and clocks, and sound recorders have all entered the list of the twenty largest export products (at the SITC 3-digit level). Even while its national average income per capita is still low – at about $400 at the current exchange rate of 8 *renminbi* per US dollar – China seems to have specialised more quickly in capital-intensive, sophisticated products.

In 1986-87, the revealed comparative advantage indices for China indicated that machinery and transport (SITC 7) were the lowest, while the highest was for the miscellaneous manufactures section (SITC 8), composed largely of labour-intensive products. In the broad machinery group of SITC 7, however, China had revealed comparative advantage only for two industries at the 3-digit SITC level: telecommunications equipment (SITC 724) and domestic electrical equipment (SITC 725). These two product groups are manufactured using relatively labour-intensive production processes, while capital-intensive procedures are employed for other SITC 7 products.

It is true that Asian NIEs and ASEAN countries also have comparative advantage for both of these products in SITC 7 (Table 2).

China's indices of revealed comparative advantage for telecommunications equipment and domestic electrical equipment are lower than Asian NIEs but higher than ASEAN countries. This indicates that at an earlier stage of nationwide economic development, China has been able to become more specialised in the export of capital-intensive machinery, although such exports are still relatively labour-intensive within that category.

It is worth noting that China has revealed comparative advantage *vis-à-vis* ASEAN countries in capital- and technology-intensive products despite a similar development stage and even lower per-capita income. China's comparative advantage in labour-intensive and natural resource-based products is essentially in relation to advanced countries and NIEs, not ASEAN countries. However, it is also interesting to note that over the past ten years, China has been gaining comparative advantage relative to NIEs in, for example, certain general industrial instruments and components (SITC 74), office machinery and automatic data processing (SITC 75), electrical products other than broadcasting equipment (SITC 77), and some road vehicles (SITC 78 and 79) (Takahashi, 1995).

China's specialisation in exports of chemical products in SITC 5 seems striking, given its stage of economic development. However, those involving comparative advantage basically consist of three resource-based products: in descending order of advantage,

Table 2. **Revealed comparative advantage indices for two products in SITC 7;
China and other ASEAN countries**

	Telecommunications equipment		Domestic electric equipment	
	1975-77	1986-87	1975-77	1986-87
China	0.08	1.27	0.11	1.09
Chinese Taipei	4.07	2.51	0.38	1.21
Hong Kong	2.54	2.04	1.51	3.19
South Korea	2.00	2.80	0.11	2.66
Singapore	2.38	3.15	0.78	1.60
Malaysia	0.68	3.54	0.07	0.57
Thailand	0.03	0.08	0.05	0.17
Indonesia	0.06	0.02	0.00	0.00
Philippines	0.08	0.21	0.00	0.19
Japan	3.51	2.54	1.11	1.12

Note: Numbers above unity indicate comparative advantage whose index is defined as the share in Chinese total exports
divided by the world share in total world exports with regard to each product.
Source: Yeats, 1991.

explosives and pyrotechnics; essential oils; and inorganic elements and oxides. There would not appear to be any particular comparative advantage in R&D-intensive or sophisticated chemical products.

IV. Trade implications of wide regional diversity

The third question is whether China's relatively early specialisation and comparative advantage in the machinery group reflects the wide diversity of regional development within China's enormous economy.

China is not an integrated economy. It is, rather, a set of provincial and regional economies separated by high resistance to trade and factor flows, with widely differing resource endowments and, hence, comparative advantages (Garnaut and Huang, 1995). What are the implications of these "multi-independent" economies within China for its position in the international division of labour?

To begin with, they will tend to support early diversification of exports toward more sophisticated products and away from simple, labour-intensive products. China's regional diversity has two features. One is magnitude: provincial disparity of per capita income is 6 to 1 and that of arable land per capita 10 to 1. The other is a high degree of isolation among major regions in terms of production factor flows, due essentially to high transportation costs in the vast country and to regional regulations. As a result, China is composed of at least three discrete economies: rapidly growing coastal areas, emerging inland areas, and underdeveloped inland regions. Each region is equipped with different natural resource, production and technology factor endowments.

The dynamic southeast coastal regions are already experiencing higher labour costs, and stronger pressure to transform production and exports into more sophisticated, capital-intensive economic activities. In contrast, low-income inland regions, with per capita income closer to Indonesia, will continue to provide coastal regions with natural resource and labour-intensive products. Coastal regions will in turn support industrialisation of inland economies through upgrading and specialisation of their own economies into, as mentioned above, more sophisticated products and services and more capital-intensive processes (Garnaut and Huang, 1995).

On top of the strong export orientation of coastal economies there is the inter-regional trade within China – which should further contribute to the upgrading of exports by coastal regions through economies of scale and scope, owing to the size of domestic markets.

In sum, China will be able to upgrade the production and export structures of its coastal regions in a manner similar to the successful dynamic transformation of Asian NIEs, but it can do so at an earlier stage of economic development than the ASEAN countries (except Singapore) despite China's low average income per capita.

V.   Trade and technology implications of economic reforms

Changed characteristics of exports

Both the rapid growth and dramatic compositional change of China's exports in the 1980s and 1990s can be attributed to economic reform – particularly since the mid-1980s. Three categories of reform are responsible for high export performance (Lardy, 1992). The first concerns decentralisation of decision-making in foreign trade. This has been confirmed by the growing number of small and medium-sized foreign trading companies established by provinces and municipalities, and the tougher competition that has ensued. The scope of state-planned exports declined to only 20 per cent of China's total exports in 1988. The second involves reforms in the pricing of traded goods. The domestic prices of 90 per cent of China's total imports were based on world market prices by the end of 1989. Thirdly, there is the abandonment of an overvalued *renminbi* exchange rate. From the first half of the 1980s to 1995, the yuan-US dollar exchange rate depreciated from 1.5-3.0 *renminbi* per dollar to 8 *renminbi* per dollar.

In creating decentralised trade based on economic incentives, these economic reforms have fundamentally altered the characteristics of China's exports in three interrelated areas: ownership of export enterprises; origin of exports by region; and product composition of exports.

By the late 1980s, the most successful and rapidly growing exporters were rural township and village enterprises and joint venture enterprises, all of which accounted for a growing share of China's exports. In provinces where these enterprises have flourished and state enterprises are less dominant, export performance has been much better. The notable example is Guandong Province, where export growth was 29 per cent per year, compared with 13 per cent for the rest of the country after 1985 – accounting for more than 20 per cent of China's total exports in the early 1990s, compared with 11 per cent in 1985. In Guandong, only one-quarter of firms were state-owned in 1988. However, export performance was poor in Shanghai, where large-scale and state-owned enterprises accounted for two-thirds of industrial output (Garnaut and Huang, 1995).

Furthermore, until the mid-1980s, China's exports were dominated by primary commodities such as grain and minerals (petroleum, coals, etc.) The share of these commodities in China's total exports has sharply declined since trade reforms were introduced in the mid-1980s. Guandong is not a significant producer of crude oil, and its arable land per capita is among the smallest (37.4 hectares per thousand people) in China (81.9 hectares).

As a result, the product composition of Chinese exports has evolved very much along the lines of comparative advantage, *i.e.* small, rural, enterprise-based, labour-intensive manufactured products. The role of foreign direct investment in Special Economic Zones (briefly discussed below), particularly Hong Kong's direct investment in southeast China, has been crucial for this development. In Guandong, for instance, indigenous enterprises and joint venture companies are equally important, accounting for half the export growth between 1985 and 1990.

Changing characteristics of technologies

The share of industrial production by non-state enterprises surpassed that of state-owned enterprises by 1992. At the present time, the latter has even been matched by the share of rural township and village enterprises; these numbered about 1.5 million and employed 51.5 million in 1992. Their national production in real terms rose by a factor of 10 between 1980 and 1992. The average number of employees per enterprise was only 34; the value-added was about 11 700 thousand yuan per worker.

The most striking example of basic technological development is the country's machine tool industry, whose scale of production already ranked China as the fifth largest (above $1.3 billion) in the world in 1993. What is worth investigating is whether efficiency is higher in rural township and village enterprises than in state-owned enterprises, and how technological development is associated with efficiency at the enterprise level.

In 1991, labour productivity in the machine tool industry as measured by value-added per employee became higher in small-scale enterprises than in medium- and large-scale state-owned enterprises, although the capital/labour ratio was still 50 to 60 per cent lower in the former than in the latter. Even in rural township and village enterprises, labour productivity was only 10 per cent or so lower than in state-owned enterprises despite very low capital/labour ratios (less than half that of the state-owned enterprises; see Otsuka, Liu and Murakami, 1995). For the machine tool industry, economies of scale at the plant level do not matter much; management and industrial organisation can be more important for efficiency.

One of the fundamental reasons for the extremely high capital/labour ratios (and the large number of employees per enterprise) in medium- and large-scale state-owned enterprises is the self-sufficiency production system, embracing all production processes from components to final products. Indeed, the outsourcing ratio of component procurement was very low at only 11.0 per cent for large-scale state enterprises and 21.6 per cent for medium-scale state enterprises in 1991. In contrast, the outsourcing ratio was high for small-scale and rural township and village enterprises, at 39.7 per cent and 39.2 per cent, respectively, in the same year (Table 3).

Japanese experience with regard to successful development of the machine tool industry suggests that the key technologies for success are not necessarily highly creative and patented, but those associated with management of product development, production process, and quality control. This incremental type of innovation is better performed by small-scale and rural township and village enterprises. Furthermore, if the outsourcing procurement of components gradually increases through loose vertical integration between machine tool producers and component suppliers – based on increasingly long-term repetitive transaction relationships – incremental innovation may be facilitated in China in a way similar to the Japanese experience. However, in order to produce better-quality components and hence machine tools, industry-supporting fundamental technolo-

Table 3. **Labour productivity, capital/labour ratio, and outsourcing ratio of components in machine-tool industry by scale and ownership of enterprise**

	1980	1985	1991
Employees (persons)			
Large-scale state enterprises (top 5)	5 919	6 261	6 111
Medium-scale state enterprises (next 6-18)	911	964	920
Small-scale enterprises (next 19-33)	328	401	395
Township and village enterprises (5)	–	–	253
Labour productivity (1 000 yuan/person)[a]			
Large-scale state enterprises	3.75	4.99	7.42
Medium-scale state enterprises	3.47	4.95	7.40
Small-scale enterprises	3.27	4.86	7.60
Township and village enterprises	–	–	6.69
Capital/labour ratio (1 000 yuan/person)[b]			
Large-scale state enterprises	12.6	14.0	21.7
Medium-scale state enterprises	10.0	10.8	16.0
Small-scale enterprises	5.8	7.2	11.9
Township and village enterprises	–	–	9.3
Outsourcing ratio of components (%)[c]			
Large-scale state enterprises	19.2	12.4	11.0
Medium-scale state enterprises	18.7	26.5	21.6
Small-scale enterprises	32.7	33.8	39.7
Township and village enterprises[a, b]	–	–	39.2

a) Value added per production worker.
b) Productive fixed asset per production worker.
c) Outsourced components divided by intermediate imports.
Source: Otsuka, Liu and Murakami, 1995.

gies such as forging, casting, moulding and plating also need to develop. Early heavy industralisation, which did not occur in other Asian developing countries, appears to provide China with greater potential for developing industry-supporting fundamental technologies.

In sum, rapid economic development in China following economic reforms and opening of the market in 1979 has been strongly facilitated by two policies. First, foreign direct investment has been attracted through the opening of coastal areas to foreign companies in Special Economic Zones. Secondly, rural township and village enterprises have been activated through agricultural reforms. The result has been an evolution of China's trade structure much more along the lines of market-based comparative advantage, and an earlier and faster upgrading of comparative advantage considering the nation's low per capita income.

VI. The new direction of technology development in China

Technology Development Zones versus Special Economic Zones

Special Economic Zones (SEZs) have been established as a means of introducing advanced technology and management know-how; development experiments are conducted in collaboration with foreign companies, and with the help of foreign technologies. This policy has brought the Chinese economy into line with the international division of labour by exposing it to international market competition. Five SEZs have been created: Shenzhen, Zhuhai, and Shanton in 1980; Xiamen in 1981; and Hainan Island in 1987. In particular, the Shenzhen Zone, adjacent to Hong Kong, has been a focal point of foreign direct investment, especially in the assembly activities of electrical and electronic components. Notable examples of the presence of Japanese companies and sophisticated products are Sanyo Electric Co. for radio cassette recorder and semiconductor assembly, Hitachi Ltd. for TV picture tube assembly, and Epson for printers.

Foreign companies have often entered Shenzhen through subcontracting the processing of products to local enterprises. An astonishing number of rural township and village enterprises have engaged in subcontracting manufacturing.

While China's open-door policy began with the establishment of such Special Economic Zones in the south, the policy then extended to all the key cities in the coastal areas after 1984; Economic and Technological Development Zones have been established in fourteen open coastal cities. These ETDZs have taken full advantage of SEZs' experiences, and have accelerated China's open market policy.

However, ETDZs differ from SEZs in several important respects (Seki, 1994).

First, while an SEZ is the proposed site of an eventual complete city, an ETDZ is an industrial area situated within a coastal city, not an independent urban area.

Secondly, sites for SEZs are chosen in underdeveloped areas, with historically weak industrial and technological bases. In contrast, sites for ETDZs are selected in historically somewhat developed areas, already equipped with certain levels of industrial, technological and (hence) economic strength. Examples of the latter are Shanghai, Tianjin, Guangzhou, Dalian, and Qingdao.

Thirdly, an SEZ provides favourable corporate income tax treatment not only for manufacturing, but also for commerce and services. An ETDZ favours only manufacturing operations affiliated with foreign companies.

Now that the benefits of both types of zones have become so evident, local governments in other areas wish to establish their own zones to attract foreign investment, offering the incentive of even lower corporate tax than favourable national rates. In these areas, local governments compensate for corporate income tax differentials.

Among the fourteen ETDZs in China's open coastal cities, the Dalian Zone (established in 1984) is the most mature, with a projected total population of 150 000 – including 50 000 workers – by the year 2000 in a 24 square kilometre site on the Dahuwan peninsula, 27 kilometres away from the Dalian city. Several hundred companies are operating there; about half are foreign companies, and half of those Japanese. Since 1990, the Japanese Industrial Park has been developed, attracting a coalition of Japanese companies including three large trading companies and two city and long-term credit banks, and also nearly one hundred small- and medium-scale Japanese enterprises. The leading manufacturing sectors include electric and electrical products, metal products, precision and medical instruments and general machinery. As a result, machinery and metal-related industrial sectors constitute a high proportion of the total. Top-ranking Japanese manufacturing companies are already in the Dalian Zone – for example, Toshiba for motor and television components, Canon for laser printers and cartridges, Star Micronics Manufacturing for printers, Sanyo Electric, and Omron.

High-tech industrial development parks and Experimental Zones

China began a state-level programme for high-tech industrial development parks in the Spring of 1991. The programme suggests that China's industrial and science and technology policies have evolved to the point where the nation is no longer seeking merely to create production bases by inviting foreign investment into the SEZs and ETDZs. Its new strategy is to move in the direction of developing industries more explicitly through the accumulation of knowledge in science and technology – and thus to go beyond the ASEAN countries' industrialisation policy of encouraging exports and inviting foreign investment. This is possible because China would seem to have an advantage over the ASEAN countries and Hong Kong in terms of the historical accumulation of both human and physical capital.

The Beijing Experimental Zone for Development of New Technology Industries (China's Silicon Valley), approved in 1988, includes leading Chinese research and academic institutions such as Beijing University, Quinghua University and the Chinese Academy of Sciences.

A notable feature of this Experimental Zone is that once either a foreign or a domestic company located there is officially recognised as a high-tech enterprise, it will receive favourable tax treatment equivalent to that accorded an SEZ. One of the qualifications for such recognition is that at least 30 per cent of the employees should be university graduates (in the context of relatively few high school graduates entering universities and colleges). Over two thousand such enterprises have already been established in the Zone, attracting the participation of professors and researchers from leading universities and research organisations.

One successful example is a firm that started as a small township enterprise in 1984 and now produces 80 per cent of all Chinese-language word processors. Employees total 3 100, 67 per cent of which are university graduates. This enterprise has extended its activities to computers and software development, and is becoming global in its scope of operation by conducting joint ventures and forming technological alliances with world-leading high-tech companies.

Another notable feature of the "Beijing Silicon Valley" is the role played by Qinghua University – China's top technical university – which is at the forefront of leading-edge technologies in machinery, electronics, biology and new materials. In 1988, this university established its own Technology Development Corporation, a private firm whose president is the university's vice-president. The corporation manufactures high-tech products on the basis of orders received from around the world, especially from US companies such as Hewlett Packard, Digital Equipment and Motorola.

The Corporation's activities reflect a new national policy meant to overcome problems in efficiently commercialising China's advanced science and technology capacity. The Corporation and Beijing's Silicon Valley are intended to play a leading role in founding high-tech sectors in China on a solid commercial "manufacturing" basis. Furthermore, the main street of Beijing's Experimental Zone is crowded with retail outlets for computers, semiconductors, electronic parts, etc. along several kilometres – an equivalent to Tokyo's busy high-tech Akihabara district.

Discussions of China's reforms and market-opening policies tend to focus on the SEZs and ETDZs in the coastal areas. Beijing's Experimental Zone differs totally from both categories. First, the SEZs – Shenzhen in particular – have primarily served as production bases for exports, utilising the skills technology and management know-how of foreign companies engaged in direct investment. In sharp contrast, industrial activities in Beijing's Experimental Zone are clearly based on China's own best and brightest scientists and engineers. Its future potential for technological development looks very bright.

Another important feature of the high-tech industrial development zones at state level is that indigenous Chinese companies are also eligible for favourable corporate tax treatment – yet another sharp contrast with the SEZs and ETDZs, where only foreign companies are accorded such treatment. Nearly thirty specified sites have been selected for Experimental Zones. Almost all of them are located in principal cities, including not only Beijing, Shanghai and Dalian but also Shenyang, Hangzhou, Hefei, Chongquing, Xi'an, etc.

More than ten years have passed since economic reform and market-opening policies were initiated, with the resulting development of coastal regions; now, the major cities of China's inlands are beginning to adopt their own approaches to regional development.

Shenyang in Liaoning Province, the largest city in northeastern China, is representative of a heavy machinery industrial base. It has the potential to become China's crucial site for an East Asian industrial and technological network, supported by the Shenyang Nanhu Science and Technology Development Zone (which emulates the Beijing Silicon Valley concept). This Zone can exploit latent industrial and technological capabilities associated with China's history of high national investment in heavy industry. In particular, the Shanxi Industrial Zone in Shenyang has a seventy-year history of heavy industries, with 420 000 semi-skilled workers and craftsman and 40 000 engineers. About 1 000 factories in the Zone, most of which are large-scale with several thousand employees, operate in basic industries such as machinery, metallurgy, chemicals, electronics, and spinning. This is a mammoth industrial area.

In addition, the Nanhu Science and Technology Development Zone, designated as a High-Tech Industrial Zone at the state level in 1991, is Shenyang's research and academic area, encompassing 12 universities, 29 research institutes and 210 large research laboratories. The Nanhu Zone resembles Beijing's Silicon Valley in that it makes full use of the Zone's – particularly Northeast University's – accumulated science and technology, commercialises that knowledge and develops industries in collaboration with domestic and foreign companies. Furthermore, there is a Science and Technology Entrepreneurs Center which serves as a business incubator by providing support for research and development activities. A venture capital organisation has also been established to provide financing for new business if needed. On the part of the Chinese Government, there has been an increasingly clear understanding of the distinction between science and technology, and that the development of science will not automatically lead to the development of technologies for manufacturing (Science, Technology and Economy Corporation, 1994). In the 1980s, many problems arose from poor manufacturing technologies, as vividly explained by Hoshino (1993).

Shenyang, as one of the key inland cities in China, is in a better geographical position to be a collection and distribution centre for the domestic market. It is also better equipped with China's own science and technology. Thus, Shenyang stands in sharp contrast to the coastal areas that are, in essence, merely processing and exporting bases.

Indeed, Shenyang will continue to contribute to technological developments in China. To begin with, it will strengthen industry-supporting fundamental technologies such as casting, forging, plating, heat treatment, painting, machining, pressing and plastic moulding. Secondly, supported by science and technology development policies, it will strengthen its high-tech sectors, and facilitate high-tech spin-offs. Thirdly, it will develop intermediate processing and assembling technologies with the help of foreign direct investment, as in the case of the ASEAN countries. These are the three basic technology layers necessary for Shenyang to become a comprehensive, well-balanced industrial base. Other areas with heavy machinery industrial bases may also hold Shenyang's promise, such as Shanghai, Chongqing, Wuhan, Xi'an and Nanjing. The 27 projects in the Xi'an Development Zone of High Technology Industries (Table 4) very clearly indicate the wide range of high-tech products to be developed in China.

Table 4. **27 projects of Xi'an Development Zone of High Technology Industries**

Content of project

1. Large-screen, multi-function display system
2. Transistor ultra-audio frequency power source
3. Outside measure liquid level meter
4. Fibre optic measure instrument
5. Miniature camera
6. Cait Bighope Chinese System with sound
7. A system of infrared warning and infrared/TV monitoring
8. Automobile electronic products
9. Silicon stack and silicon bridge of large current series
10. Laserdisc production line
11. Video doorphone
12. Electronic lamp with magic and kaleidoscope
13. Optical composing colour photograph and characters machine
14. ATS Series automatic target scoring system
15. Fully automatic integrated
16. Mobile quick position and tracking system for vehicles
17. Process total distributed control system
18. Thin welded pipe plated with tin-lead
19. High-quality automobile piston
20. Ceramic composite inserts with high strength and high resistance
21. Boiling suspension kiln
22. FBT (rare earth) series of compound thermal insulation and energy-saving material
23. SKB series of intelligent controlled highly burglar-resistant safes
24. Family video camera
25. Wire-wireless-wire converter
26. JDJ (rare-earth) coating for thermal insulation
27. Xanthan Gum Production Line with annual capacity of 1 000 tons

Source: Administrative Committee of Xi'an Development Zone of High Technology Industries, 1994.

VII. Conclusions and implications for OECD countries

China appears to differ in technological structure and industrial development from the ASEAN countries, and also probably from NIEs.

A nation desiring to build solid manufacturing capabilities must establish a structure of industry and technology that is necessarily multi-layered and complex. To shed light on the interaction between technology and comparative advantage, it is useful to simplify the complex structure of technology into just three layers: 1) industry-supporting fundamental technologies; 2) high technologies; and 3) assembly technologies lying somewhere between the two (Seki, 1994).

The fundamental technologies at the base of the structure consist of casting, forging, plating, heat treatment, painting, machining, pressing, plastic moulding, and other process technologies. In the case of Japan, small and medium-sized enterprises have built up fundamental manufacturing technologies in order to respond to both the stringent quality demands of customers (*e.g.* large-scale enterprises) and intense price competition. In China, small-scale and rural township and village enterprises will grow to develop such fundamental technologies in the twenty-first century.

At the apex of industrial technology are the special or high technologies focusing on new product development, often unique to the enterprise concerned. These special technologies are usually developed by large private corporations.

Much of high-tech is based on digital electronic technology, whereas most of the fundamental technologies are analog and mechanical. The latter require a craftsman's skill, which takes years of learning to acquire. Possession (or lack) of such fundamental technologies will have a strong influence on the industrial development of a country or a region.

In the middle layer between the fundamental and high technologies are the intermediate technologies linking the two. A good example is assembly technology.

The ASEAN countries and, similarly, Hong Kong are weak in both high-tech and industry-supporting fundamental technologies. The colonial history of these countries has made it difficult for them to develop and establish an independent industrial base. Over the past ten to fifteen years, the ASEAN countries have encouraged assembly sectors through inviting foreign direct investment. Foreign companies have brought their own established technologies and production facilities and components into host countries, and combined them with plentiful inexpensive local workers for simple assembly work. Although ASEAN countries have achieved economic growth and industrialisation, they have not yet been successful in building an independent technology base for further industrial development. Singapore seems to have followed an industrialisation strategy, placing a high priority on developing high technologies (biotechnology, biomedicine, computer and information technology, microelectronics, chemical engineering, etc.) by relocating to neighbouring countries low value-added assembly sectors. However, Singapore is not developing industry-supporting fundamental technologies.

China has a unique potential to develop sophisticated technology-intensive products at an earlier stage of development due to its long history of investing in capital- and technology-intensive industries as well as in human capital. Of course, some of these investments involved a misallocation of resources. However, once human capital investments and accumulated knowledge are effectively utilised for commercial production and services, they become the source of comparative advantage, at least at the margin of producing and exporting certain capital- and technology-intensive manufactured products. This source of comparative advantage is not available to ASEAN countries or even to Asian NIEs.

Successful industrialisation requires the above-mentioned three-layered, properly balanced structure of these three different technologies. China will probably be able to achieve that balance in the twenty-first century, for the above-mentioned reasons.

On the basis of reasonable assumptions about the growth of China (8 per cent), Japan (3 per cent) and the world economy (3 per cent), and about trends in each country's trade/GDP ratio (*e.g.* some increase in China's total trade/GDP ratio, a large increase in Japan's imports/GDP ratio), China will export almost twice as much as Japan in the year 2015. China's share of world trade in that year could be around 13.4 per cent, while Japan's share will be considerably smaller, around 10.6 per cent. This turnaround in favour of China is particularly astonishing when compared with 1994, when Japan's share of world exports was 10.4 per cent, 3.2 times as large as China's share at 3.3 per cent (Song and Zhao, 1995).

The accommodation of continuing, rapid, export-oriented growth in China is one of the greatest challenges facing the world economy over the next few decades. Since the reforms, growing complementarity in the industrial structure between capital- and technology-rich advanced countries and labour-rich China has induced strong growth of labour-intensive manufactured exports from China to advanced countries in exchange for capital- and technology-intensive exports from advanced countries to China.

Global adjustment to the rapid expansion of Chinese labour-intensive exports has been facilitated by two developments: a rapid fall in the world share of such exports from Japan up to the mid-1980s; and a rapid fall in the world share of such exports from NIEs after the mid-1980s. The increase in China's share came at the same time as the rapid rise of South-East Asia's role in world trade in these products. Yet, the total share of world exports of labour-intensive products from East Asia (NIEs plus ASEAN) has hardly risen since the mid-1980s (Garnaut and Huang, 1995).

On the one hand, as China's trade shifts from labour-intensive to capital- and technology-intensive manufactured products, there will be more direct competition with even the highly industrialised countries. On the other hand, advanced countries will benefit if China's trade structure incorporates greater intra-industry trade. Another positive factor is that China's imports are much higher than they would have been in the absence of economic reforms – according to one estimate, by 92 per cent, or $36 billion, in 1992 after a decade of reform (Song and Zhao, 1995).

In the distant future, the adjustment challenge could be as large as that presented by the emergence of Japan at a similar stage of economic development. In the forthcoming ten to fifteen years, however, the trade tension between China and advanced countries will be less contentious than was the case with Japan after the 1970s, assuming that China becomes a member of WTO rather soon. First, China's overall external trade account will be more or less balanced, due to high growth and high domestic investment that will continue to absorb high domestic saving. Chinese imports will continue to grow rapidly in parallel with Chinese exports on a cyclically adjusted basis. Japan's external surplus became persistent only after 1970, when the growth rate slowed from high (at more than 10 per cent per year) to medium (at 4 to 5 per cent) while the domestic saving rate remained high. Secondly, China's intra-industry trade could prove greater than Japan's. The latter country's natural resource endowments are so poor that its comparative advantage structure has been characterised by predominant imports of primary commodities and by predominant exports of manufactured products, leaving little room for manufactured trade (including intra-industry), particularly with highly industrialised countries. In sharp contrast, China is enormously rich in natural resources. China's imports will continue to be dominated by manufactured products. Thirdly, China is strongly committed to inward foreign direct investment (FDI), whereas Japan essentially banned inward FDI until the end of the 1970s. The result will be a substantial amount of production and services provided by multinational companies in China in addition to their licensing fees and export proceeds from the country, a situation very much in these companies' interests. Thus the three sources of trade and investment tension between Japan and other advanced countries will not likely become causes of serious tension between China and partner OECD countries.

Indeed, the nature of trade conflict between China and its trading partners will probably become more like that between the European Community and the United States, rather than like that between Japan and the United States.

Bibliography

ADMINISTRATIVE COMMITTEE OF XI'AN DEVELOPMENT ZONE OF HIGH TECHNOL-
OGY INDUSTRIES (1994), "Projects of Technical Cooperation with Foreign Countries in XDZ".

GARNAUT, Ross and Yiping HUANG (1995), "China in Transition: Opportunities and Challenges for OECD Countries", Report prepared for the OECD Trade Directorate, Paris.

GROVES, T., Y. HONG, J. McMILLAN and B. NAUGHTON (1995), "China's Evolving Managerial Labor Market", *Journal of Political Economy*, Vol. 103, No. 4, pp. 873-889.

LARDY, R. (1992), "Chinese Foreign Trade", *The China Quarterly*, Vol. 92.

LARDY, R. (1994), *China in the World Economy*, Institute for International Economics, Washington, DC.

LAU, Lawrence J. (1994), "The Chinese Economy in the Twenty-First Century", Stanford University, mimeo.

SONG, Ligang and Shiji ZHAO (1995), "Issues in the China-Japan Trade Relationship", Australia-Japan Research Center, Research School of Pacific and Asian Studies, Australian National University, Canberra.

WORLD BANK (1994), *China: Foreign Trade Reform*, World Bank Country Study, Washington, DC.

YEATS, Alexander J. (1991), "China's Foreign Trade and Comparative Advantage: Prospects, Problems, and Policy Implications", World Bank Discussion Papers, No. 141.

In Japanese

HOSHINO, Yoshiro (1993), "Technology and Politics", Nihon Hyoron Sha, Tokyo.

OTSUKA, K., T. LIU and N. MURAKAMI (1995), "Micro-Economic Reforms in China: Quantitative Analysis of Firms and Markets", Nihon Keizai Shimbun, Tokyo.

SCIENCE, TECHNOLOGY AND ECONOMY CORPORATION (1994), "The Current State of Dynamically Growing Chinese Industries and Future Perspective", Report prepared by the Study Groups of Chinese Techno-Economics.

SEKI, Mitsuhiko (1994), "Beyond the Full-Set Industrial Structure: Japanese Industry in the New Age of East Asia", Chuo Koron Sha, Tokyo.

TAKAHASHI, Hiroshi (1995), "International Competitiveness Structure of China by Her Trading Partner Country", *Journal of Tokyo International University* (edited by the Department of Economics), No. 12.

China's Food Economy: Past Performance and Future Trends

Justin Yifu Lin
Director
China Center for Economic Research
University of Beijing

Jikun Huang
Professor and Director
Center for Chinese Agricultural Policy
Agricultural Economics Institute
Chinese Academy of Agricultural Sciences

and

Scott Rozelle
Assistant Professor
Food Research Institute, Stanford University

I. Introduction

Since economic reforms began in the late 1970s, China's overall economic growth rate has been remarkable (Table 1). The replacement of the collective farming system by a household-based system over the period 1978-84 improved farmers' incentives and made agriculture the leading growth sector. Then in the mid-1980s, as the one-off efficiency gains from the institutional reform of farming were essentially exhausted, agriculture's growth rate decelerated. Meanwhile, because of reforms in the urban area, growth rates in other sectors continued to accelerate. The industrial and service sectors' growth rates each almost tripled, from about 6 per cent in the early period of reforms to about 16 per cent by the early 1990s.

The rapid economic development has been accompanied by dramatic changes in economic structure (Table 2). As a result of bold trade liberalisation, China's foreign trade grew much faster than national income. The value of exports relative to national income rose from 3 per cent in 1970 to 7 per cent in 1980 and 20 per cent in 1992, a

Table 1. **Growth rates (%) of national income by sector**[a]

	Pre-reform 1970-78	Reform period			
		1978-84	1984-90	1990-92	1978-92
National income	4.9	7.9	8.6	11.0	9.0
Agriculture	2.7	11.5	6.0	1.7	7.6
Industry	6.8	5.9	9.4	15.1	8.9
Others	4.6	5.8	11.8	16.9	12.3
Population	1.9	1.2	1.7	1.2	1.4
Per capita national income	3.0	6.7	6.8	9.7	7.5

a) Growth rates are computed using the regression method.
Source: ZGTJNJ (Statistical Yearbook of China), 1993.

Table 2. **Changes in the structure of China's economy (%)**

	1970[a]	1980	1985	1990	1992
Rural share in total population	83	81	76	74	72
Share in national income					
Agriculture	41	37	37	33	29
Crops		73	64	57	56
Livestock		18	21	27	27
Fishery		2	4	6	7
Forestry		4	5	4	5
Sideline		4	6	6	6
Industry	46	53	51	53	56
Services	13	10	14	15	15
Share in employment					
Agriculture	81	69	62	60	59
Industry	10	18	21	21	22
Services	9	13	17	19	20
Share in exports					
Agriculture	37	19	18	13	12
Processed agriculture	38	29	29	29	n.a.
Industry and others	25	52	53	58	n.a.
Share in imports					
Agriculture	n.a.	34	14	16	11
Manufacture and others	n.a.	66	86	84	89
Export ratio to national income	3	7	11	16	20

n.a.: Not available.
a) These are 3-year averages centred at year shown.
Source: Huang and David, 1995.

threefold increase during the reform period. Judged by the trade dependence ratio, China had become the most open of the world's large economies by the early 1990s. On the other hand, agriculture's share in the national economy has declined, from 41 per cent of national income in 1970 to 29 per cent in 1992. At the same time, agriculture's share in total exports fell from 37 per cent to 12 per cent, and its share in total employment declined from 81 per cent to 59 per cent. Within agriculture, the composition of gross domestic product also changed, with the share of crops – specifically grains, oil, cotton, and other cash crops – declining in favour of livestock, fisheries, and other commodities. Among crops, the growth rate of grain production, after reaching its historical peak in the early reform period, has suffered a rapid decline (Table 3). Partly due to the slow growth, severe grain price hikes were observed in the Autumn of 1993, and more recently from May 1994 to early 1995.

The future of China's grain economy has been the subject of concern both within and outside China. A number of grain forecasters have claimed that China's grain imports will increase significantly in the near future. For example, Brown (1994) states that China's grain imports will exceed 200 million metric tonnes (MMT) by 2030, a rapid increase that will strain the world's productive capacity. However, most of China's own economists disagree. Researchers in the Chinese Academy of Agricultural Sciences have long predicted, and still believe, that the nation will maintain a high level of self-

Table 3. **Growth rates (%) of crop production, sown area and yields in China, 1970-92**

Commodity	Pre-reform	Reform period		
	1970-78	1978-84	1984-92	1978-92
Grain				
Production	2.8	4.7	1.8	2.7
Sown area	0.0	−1.1	0.1	−0.5
Yield	2.8	5.8	1.7	3.2
Rice				
Production	2.5	4.5	1.3	2.3
Sown area	0.7	−0.6	−0.0	−0.4
Yield	1.8	5.1	1.3	2.7
Other grain				
Production	3.1	4.8	2.2	2.9
Sown area	−0.2	−1.3	0.2	−0.5
Yield	3.3	6.1	2.0	3.4
Cash crops				
Real output	2.1	14.9	2.3	6.3
Sown area	2.4	5.1	2.0	3.4

Note: Growth rates are computed using the regression method. See data section for computation of real output value for cash crops.
Source: ZGTJNJ (1980-93).

sufficiency. The future growth of grain production could be accelerated by an increase in grain yield through technological innovation, especially relating to seed improvement (Lin, 1994, 1995; Mei, 1995). Whatever course China's grain economy takes, the stakes are high for the country's development and for the stability and health of the world's agricultural trade. The purpose of this paper is to assess the performance of China's agriculture in the past decades and to project the future growth of China's food supply and demand balances. Section II provides an overview of the growth of grain production and the forces underlying this growth. Structural changes in food consumption are presented in the third section. Then in Section IV, food demand and supply projections are made using a model recently developed by Huang, Rozelle and Rosegrant (1995). In this model, a series of important structural factors and policy variables are accounted for explicitly, including urbanisation and market development on the demand side, and technology, agricultural investment, environmental trends and institutional innovations on the supply side. Finally, the conclusions and implications are presented in Section V.

II. Agricultural production growth and underlying factors

The growth of agricultural production in China since the 1950s has been one of the main accomplishments of the nation's development policies. Except during the famine years of the late 1950s and early 1960s, the country has enjoyed rates of production growth that have outpaced the rise in population. Even between 1970 and 1978, when much of the economy was reeling from the effects of the Cultural Revolution, grain production grew at 2.8 per cent per annum (Table 3).[1] Rice yields grew at 1.8 per cent per year and those of other grain even faster, at 3.3 per cent. These growth rates were further accelerated during the first period of rural reform (1978-84): rice production increased by 4.5 per cent per year, and the output of other grains rose by 4.8 per cent. Yields of wheat and corn grew faster still. The most spectacular growth was enjoyed by cash crops, which expanded in real value terms by 14.9 per cent annually. However, these high growths were halted in the post-reform period. Declines in the growth of grain production after the mid-1980s, and especially since the early 1990s, have raised national concerns about future grain deficits.

Past studies have already demonstrated that there are a number of factors which might simultaneously have contributed to agricultural productivity growth during the reform period. The earliest empirical investigations by McMillan, Whalley and Zhu (1989), Fan (1991) and Lin (1992) centred around measuring the contribution of organisational reforms to agricultural growth in the early 1980s. They found that intro-duction of the household responsibility system (HRS) was a major source of output growth in agriculture. While confirming the important impacts of the institutional, price and market reforms on agricultural output growth in the early 1980s, Huang and Rozelle (forthcoming) and Huang, Rosegrant and Rozelle (1995) demonstrated that technology adoption (change) was the most important determinant of agricultural growth during the entire reform period, especially in the later stages (after 1984). The decline in the growth rate of agricultural production since the mid-1980s has been associated with the comple-tion of one-off effects of HRS, the adverse impact of price policies, the slowdown in

74

technological changes, and degradation of natural resources (Lin, 1992; Sicular, 1995; Huang, Rosegrant and Rozelle, 1995; Huang and Rozelle, 1995a). Despite the relatively high yield of grain in China, the return on agricultural research and the potential grain yield are still high (Lin, 1995).

Growth in the pre-reform period

While there were some real gains from agricultural technology in the pre-reform era, the expansion of inputs generated much of the growth in production (Perkins and Yusuf, 1984). Irrigation expanded dramatically during the 1960s and 1970s, as did the use of chemical fertilizers (ZGTJNJ, 1984). Labour was pushed intensively onto the land (Weins, 1982). After accounting for the utilisation of major inputs, the growth of total factor productivity is generally considered to have been relatively low if not zero (Wen, 1993; Tang, 1984). These low rates also dampened the real increases in rural incomes (Lardy, 1983).

Reforms in the past decade

To overcome some of the above problems, a series of reforms were launched in the late 1970s. For example, the household responsibility system, which restored the primacy of the individual household in place of the collective production team system as the basic unit of production and management in rural China, has been in place since the late 1970s (Lin, 1988). Under HRS, collectively owned land was assigned to individual households with a contract for up to fifteen years, recently extended to fifty years. The HRS has impacts not only on the incentive system, but also on the adoption of new technologies (Lin, 1991; Huang and Rozelle, forthcoming). On the other hand, China's policy-makers recognise the role of prices and market competition in determining production and efficient allocation of resources. Price and market reforms, therefore, have been key components of the country's development thrust as it gradually shifts from a socialist to a market-oriented economy. While the institutional transformation from a collective to a household responsibility system of farm management was essentially completed by the early 1980s, the process of price and market reform has still not been completed after one-and-a-half decades. Although there has definitely been a decisive trend towards liberalisation, the process has been characterised by cycles of deregulation and reinstatement of controls (Findlay et al., 1993; Lin, 1994; Huang and David, 1995; Rozelle, Park and Huang, 1995).

Recent price and market reforms

Although both the state distribution and procurement systems were liberalised in the early 1990s, the price and marketing reform process has slowed considerably since early 1994 and even slipped back as a result of the severe grain price hikes mentioned above. Some claim that the grain price inflation is mainly a result of "mis-operation" by the state Grain Bureau. Although fully committed to profit maximisation, it retained its monopsony and monopoly power in the grain market. It therefore favoured the options of either closing the grain market and forcing trade into the former centralised "main channels", or completely liberalising the grain market. Some believe that stockpiling by both government and farmers was the cause of the grain price increase in the early 1990s, while others claim that the increase was mainly driven by market forces. By end of 1994, China found itself either pushing toward or being pushed into a new phase where the market was expected to play a bigger role in sectoral resource allocation and distribution of income.

Moreover, as a result of continuing decline in the growth of grain production (Table 3), nationwide concern about a possible shortage of grain in the coming years has begun to grow. In response, several new policies have been implemented since late 1994. Grain exports were banned. Government grain procurement once again became compulsory. The procurement decisions are strictly and directly determined by the government at central and provincial levels; procurement prices are strictly determined by the central government. Market procurement of grain by non-grain bureaus is precluded until the target of 90 million tons of state grain procurement is met. Moreover, regional (provincial) grain self-sufficiency policy was reintroduced.

Technology changes

Besides the institutional, price and market reforms, many other sharp transitions are also under way. Above all, technological change has been the engine of China's agricultural economy growth (Stone, 1988), and will continue to be the main source of grain yield growth in the future (Huang, Rosegrant and Rozelle, 1995). China's technological base grew rapidly during both the pre-reform and reform periods. For example, hybrid rice, a breakthrough pioneered by Chinese rice scientists in the 1970s, increased yields significantly in many parts of the country, and rapidly spread to nearly one-half of China's rice area by 1990 (Lin, 1991; Huang and Rozelle, forthcoming). Other grains enjoyed similar technological transformations (Stone, 1988). China's robust growth in the stock of research capital has in significant part been responsible for these dramatic changes (Fan and Pardey, 1992; Huang, Rosegrant and Rozelle, 1995). There is concern, however, that China's system may be suffering from neglect after more than a decade of reform (Conroy, 1987; Lin, 1995; Pray, Rozelle and Huang, 1995). Real annual expenditures on agricultural research fell between 1985 and 1990, before resuming real growth in 1990 (SSTC, 1993). The slowdown in growth in annual investments in the late 1980s will result in slower growth in the overall stock of research in the 1990s. The ability of China's research system to maintain a stream of technical innovations will critically affect the growth of grain supply and the nation's grain balance. However, the reforms in the rest of the economy, which had resulted in more competition and shrinking fiscal revenues of central government, have put pressure on national leaders to search for ways to encourage investment in agricultural research and infrastructure.

Investment policy

Investment in agricultural infrastructure, especially irrigation, is another important determinant of China's agricultural growth in recent decades (Nickum, 1982). Irrigation investment and the stock of facilities have followed patterns similar to those for research (Huang and David, 1995). Since the early 1950s, China has invested heavily in irrigation, raising the proportion of irrigated land from 18 per cent of cultivated area to nearly one-half (ZGTJNJ, 1993). Real annual expenditures on irrigation rose rapidly until 1975, before beginning a ten-year decline. However, in 1985, annual expenditures began to grow again, and were at an all-time high in 1992 (Huang and David, 1995).

Natural resources

Trends in environmental degradation, including erosion, salinisation, and loss of cultivated land, show that there may be considerable stress on the agricultural land base: erosion and salinisation have increased since the 1970s, although in a somewhat erratic pattern (Huang and Rozelle, 1995*a*). These factors have been shown to affect output of grain, rice, and other agricultural products in a number of recent studies (Huang and Rozelle, 1995*a* and forthcoming; Rozelle, Huang and Veeck, forthcoming; Huang, Rosegrant and Rozelle, 1995).

III. Structural changes in food consumption patterns

In the rapidly growing Chinese economy, aggregate (national-level) per capita direct consumption of cereal as food has not increased as much in recent years as in the past decade, while meat, fish, and dairy consumption have increased dramatically. Typically, economists have tried to explain such changes in food consumption patterns primarily by increases in disposable income and changes in food prices. There is no doubt that household income and food prices strongly influence food consumption patterns. This fact is perhaps as well substantiated empirically as any relationship in the economics literature. Nevertheless, in examining and projecting food demand patterns over the long run, particularly in economies undergoing rapid structural transformation and urbanisation such as is expected to occur in China over the next twenty-five years,[2] it becomes clear that changes in tastes and lifestyles are also important influences on food demand.

There are a number of reasons for thinking that structural shifts (as distinguished from income and price effects) occur in food demand patterns as populations move from rural to urban areas (Huang and Bouis, 1996):

1. There is a wider choice of foods available in urban markets.
2. Urban residents are more exposed to the rich variety of dietary patterns of foreign cultures.
3. Urban lifestyles may place a premium on foods which require less time to prepare.

4. Urban occupations tend to be more sedentary, and consumers require a lower energy expenditure and so a lower calorie intake.
5. Urban residents typically do not grow their own food; thus, their consumption choices are not constrained by the potentially high-cost alternative of selling one's food at farmgate prices (say, rice) to buy other food (say, bread) at retail prices – a choice faced by semi-subsistence producers.

Within the urban sector, recent changes in the urban economy have made urban consumers almost entirely dependent on markets for their consumption needs. In this sector, prices and income changes most likely will be the fundamental force driving consumption pattern changes. Urban incomes rose at a steady rate of nearly 8 per cent per year in the early years of reform (ZGTJNJ). Rising incomes meant higher demand for almost all food products, including fine grains like wheat and rice. Real income per capita for urban residents has continued to rise in recent years, jumping an average of 5 to 7 per cent between 1985 and 1992. At the current average level of income for most urban residents, food grain consumption rises very little with new increments in income; meat consumption, on the other hand, is still very much influenced by income changes (Carter and Funing, 1991; Huang and Bouis, 1996).

Rural residents live in a very different environment than their urban counterparts, and exhibit different demand behaviour. While rural incomes have grown much more slowly since the mid-1980s, demand for food grains and meat products has still increased as incomes have risen (Huang and Rozelle, 1994, 1995b; Fan, Wailes and Cramer, 1995). Rural consumption markets also are less complete. Farmers in many areas face limited choices in their consumption decisions since many of the products they desire on a daily basis, such as meat and fresh fruit, are not always available, even when their incomes rise (Huang and Rozelle, 1995b). Discontinuous free markets, lack of refrigeration, and generally high transaction costs for procuring food in rural areas have been shown to fundamentally affect the consumption patterns of rural consumers in China. While changes in the rural market have been rapid, in 1992 Chinese farmers still purchased only 46 per cent of the food they consumed (ZGTJNJ). As markets develop, and activity on rural consumption markets increases, not only will there be changes in income and prices, but consumption patterns will also be affected.

IV. Results of food demand and supply projections

Various attempts have been made to project future trends in China's grain imports and exports. The most striking feature of the projections with regard to surpluses and deficits is their wide range. At one extreme, China is predicted to become a net exporter of grain. CAAS (1985) forecasts that China will have the capacity to export 47 MMT in the year 2000. Other analysts believe China will eventually become a net importer of grain. Brown forecasts that a rapidly modernising China will import at least 216 MMT by 2030 even if per capita consumption of grain does not increase. Other analysts also predict China's grain imports will increase significantly.

However, almost all of the changes in the future growth of supply predicted in the previous studies are dependent on assumed changes in technology (even though this process of technical change is not always explicitly recognised). Demand growth mostly depends on changes in income (and somewhat on the impact of price changes). Fundamental forces in the economy, such as urbanisation and market development as mentioned above, are ignored in most studies. Given the rapid structural change in China's economy, this omission is most likely a reflection of the poorly developed empirical literature on China's food economy. There is also little scope for assessing the impact of policy variables. With the exception of the World Bank's model, no model can be used to systematically assess the effect of policy tools that are under the control of government.

This study applies a food demand and supply projection model developed by Huang, Rozelle and Rosegrant (1995). The explanation of the model and assumptions are reported in the Annex and Annex Tables 1-3.

Results of baseline projections (Table 4)

Per capita food grain consumption in China hit its peak in the late 1980s and early 1990s. According to our projection, food grain consumption per capita falls from its baseline high of 225 kilograms over the forecast period. The average rural resident will consume greater amounts through the year 2000, before reducing food grain demand in the first decade of the next century. This decline in the rural area occurs at a time when income elasticities, although lower than in the late 1990s, are still positive. As markets develop, rural consumers have more choice, and will move away from food grains. Urban food grain consumption per capita declines over the entire projection period.

In contrast, per capita demand for red meat is forecast to rise sharply throughout the projection period. China's consumers will more than double their consumption by 2020, from 17 to 43 kilograms per capita. Rural demand will grow more slowly than overall demand, but urbanisation trends will shift more people into the higher-consuming urban areas (in 1991 an urban resident consumed about 60 per cent more red meat than his/her rural counterpart). While starting from a lower level, per capita demand for poultry and fish rise proportionally more.

The projected rise in demand for meat, poultry, fish and other animal products will put pressure on aggregate feed grain demand. In the baseline scenario, demand for feed grain will increase to 109 MMT by the year 2000. Although China does not publish aggregate feed grain statistics, by the authors' calculations this represents an increase of 30 per cent during the 1990s (up from 76 MMT in 1991). By the year 2020, the projected grain needed for feed will reach 232 MMT. At this rate of growth, feed grain as a proportion of total grain utilisation will move from 20 per cent in 1991 to 38 per cent in 2020. This process of moving from an agricultural economy that produces grain primarily for food to one which is becoming increasingly animal feed-oriented is typical of rapidly developing economies elsewhere in the world, and has been predicted by others (Carter and Funing, 1991) to occur in China also.

When considered with the projected population rates, the projected per capita demands for food and feed grain imply that aggregate grain demand in China will reach

Table 4. **Baseline projection of demand, supply and net import in China, 1991-2020**

Commodity	1991	2000	2010	2020
	Per capita food consumption (kg)			
Grain	225	223	214	203
Rural	242	246	243	239
Urban	178	177	174	168
Red meat	17	23	32	43
Rural	15	20	26	33
Urban	24	30	40	52
Poultry	2	3	5	8
Rural	1	2	3	4
Urban	4	6	8	12
Fish	6	10	17	28
Rural	4	6	9	14
Urban	12	18	28	43
	Grain demand, production and net import (MMT)			
Total grain demand	386	450	513	594
Feed demand	76	109	158	232
Domestic production	385	410	469	552
Net import	3	40	43	43

Note: Net import differs from the gap between demand and production because of the changes in stock.
Source: Huang, Rozelle and Rosegrant, 1995; authors' projections.

450 MMT by the year 2000, an increase of 17 per cent over the level of the early 1990s (386 MMT).[3]

Although per capita food demand is falling in the later projection period, total grain demand continues to increase through 2020 – mainly because of population growth and the increasing importance of meat, poultry and fish in the average diet. By the end of the forecast period, aggregate grain demand will reach 594 MMT, over 50 per cent higher than the initial baseline demand.

Baseline projections of the supply of grain show that China's producing sector gradually falls behind the increases in demand. Aggregate grain supply is projected to reach 410 MMT (in trade weight) by the year 2000. This implies a rise in grain output of only about 6.5 per cent over the early 1990s, a figure far below the more optimistic estimates given in recent years by MOA officials who had hoped to meet the target of 455 MMT by 2000 (or 500 MMT in nontrade weight figures).

On the other hand, production is expected to rise somewhat faster in the second and third decades of the forecast period. Mostly as a result of the resumption of investment in agricultural research during the forecast period, aggregate grain production is expected to reach 469 MMT in 2010, an increase of 14 per cent during the preceding ten years; production will reach 552 by 2020, an even higher percentage increase for the decade (18 per cent over the 2010 level).

Under the projected baseline scenario, the gap between the forecast annual growth rate of production and demand implies a rising deficit. Total grain consumption rises at 1.72 per cent per year, 1.28 per cent of which stems from the rise in population and 0.44 per cent from rising per capita grain demand. Nearly all of this increased per capita grain demand is from the higher demand for feed grain (it rises by 2.71 per cent while aggregate demand for food is stagnant). Grain production during this period grows only 0.64 per cent annually. Imports surge in the late 1990s to 40 MMT. After peaking in 2010 at 43 MMT, grain imports remain at that level through 2020.

Alternative projections

To test the sensitivity of the baseline results to changes in the underlying forces driving the supply and demand balances, a number of alternative scenarios are run, altering the baseline growth rates of the key variables, including population, income, feeding efficiency and non-staple food trade policy on the demand side, and investments in technology and irrigation, price policy, natural resources, and opportunity costs of labour and land on the supply side. The results, shown in Table 5, indicate that low population growth rates would reduce grain demand by 5 MMT in 2000 and 33 MMT in 2020 compared to the baseline. With high population growth, demand for grain increases to 621 MMT. Low income growth causes a decline in projected total grain demand from 594 to 549 MMT, resulting in slight exports of grain in 2020. With rapid income growth, projected demand would increase by 53 MMT. Changes in the feeding efficiency of livestock and fish production, compared to the baseline projection, would increase or decrease the demand for grain by only about 2 to 3 MMT in 2000, by 7 to 8 MMT in 2010 and 16 to 17 MMT in 2020.

Perhaps the most important result shown in Table 5 is the very large impact of income growth on demand for feed grain. This is expected, as the income elasticities of demand for meat and fish products are high.

Table 6 shows the projections of grain production under alternative assumptions of investment in research and irrigation, grain price, natural resource changes and the opportunity costs of labour and land. The most important results of this exercise are the very large impacts of investment in agricultural research and irrigation on grain production. This is hardly surprising, given the large contribution that agricultural research – and the technology it has produced – has made to agricultural productivity in recent years. Increases in the rate of growth in investment in agricultural research and irrigation from 3 to 4 per cent per year are projected to shift China from an import to an export position by 2020. If, instead, growth in annual investment in the agricultural research system and irrigation fell only moderately, from 3 per cent per year (as forecast under the baseline projections) to 2 per cent, by 2020 total production would only be 486 MMT, far below the baseline projections of grain demand and production. Table 6 also shows that grain production is insensitive to small changes in price trends. Output price trends do

Table 5. **Projections of demand for total and feed grains (MMT) under alternative scenarios in China, 1991-2020**

Alternative scenario	1991	2000	2010	2020
Baseline				
Total grain	386	450	513	594
Feed	76	109	158	232
Low population growth				
Total grain	386	445	496	561
Feed	76	108	153	218
High population growth				
Total grain	386	454	527	621
Feed	76	110	163	242
Low income growth				
Total grain	386	440	489	549
Feed	76	103	139	189
High income growth				
Total grain	386	459	537	647
Feed	76	116	181	286
Low feeding efficiency				
Total grain	386	452	520	610
Feed	76	111	165	248
High feeding efficiency				
Total grain	386	448	505	577
Feed	76	107	150	215
Import meat/feed by 10%				
Total grain	386	439	497	571
Feed	76	98	142	209

Note: See Annex Table 2 for assumptions on growth rates of income and population. High (low) feeding efficient scenario assumes that the annual growth of feeding efficiency is 0.25% higher (lower) than the baseline assumptions.
Source: Huang, Rozelle and Rosegrant, 1995; authors' projections.

affect China's grain balances, but the effects are small. At the baseline level, for every 0.5 per cent increase (decline) in the annual projected grain price trend, imports fall (rise) by 2 MMT.[4] In the total, altering assumptions on the output prices would only change the grain production from the baseline's projection by 7 to 8 MMT in 2020, because the increase in production of the one grain resulting from its own-price impact would be partially offset by the cross-price effects of the other grain.

Finally, while the production projections are sensitive to the alternative assumptions of natural resource and opportunity costs of labour and agricultural land, the difference between these projections and baseline projections is still lower than the net import of grain implied by the baseline projection (Table 4), ranging from 22 to 29 MMT.

Table 7 shows the net import requirements of grain implied by the various scenarios described above. Most of the projections show that China's grain production will gradu-

Table 6. **Projections of grain production (MMT) under alternative scenarios in China, 1991-2020**

Alternative scenario	1991	2000	2010	2020
Baseline	385	410	469	552
Investment in research and irrigation				
Low (2% per year)	385	408	441	486
High (4% per year)	385	412	500	627
World price impact				
Large (0% per year)	385	411	474	559
Small (–1% per year)	385	408	465	544
Salinity and erosion				
Improve (–0.5% per year)	385	415	481	574
Degradation (1.0% per year)	385	404	456	527
Opportunity costs of labour and land				
No change (0% per year)	385	416	486	580
High (2% per year)	385	403	454	523

Note: See Annex Table 3 for assumptions on growth rates.
Source: Huang, Rozelle and Rosegrant, 1995; authors' projections.

ally fall behind the increases in demand. Imports will rise significantly before the year 2000. Low population growth would reduce grain demand, with total grain imports falling to only 9 MMT. With high population growth, imports increase to 70 MMT. Low income growth leads to a decline in projected grain demand and results in slight exports of grain in 2020. With rapid income growth, projected imports would more than double, to 96 MMT. While net imports of grain are less sensitive to assumptions relating to feeding efficiency, prices, salinity, erosion and opportunity costs of labour and land, they are highly sensitive to changes in government investment in research and irrigation. With no change in the assumption regarding the level of food demand, China could become a grain net exporter after 2010 if the growth rate of investment in research and irrigation reaches 4 per cent per year. On the other hand, if the growth in annual investment in agricultural research and irrigation fell from the baseline of 3 per cent per year, by 2020 imports under such a scenario would reach a level of 106 MMT.

This level of grain imports could be expected only if there were continued decline in the growth of agricultural investment, and if the government did not respond with countervailing policy measures as import levels rose. Such a scenario could unfold only if the government was unwilling or unable to undertake policies to stimulate food production growth. However, agricultural research and irrigation investments have already recovered in recent years, and in recent months, as grain prices have risen in response to

Table 7. **Projections of grain net import (MMT) under alternative scenarios in China, 1991-2020**

Alternative scenario	1991	2000	2010	2020
Baseline	3	40	43	43
Population growth				
Low	3	35	26	9
High	3	45	57	70
Income growth				
Low	3	30	20	–2
High	3	49	67	96
Feeding efficiency				
Low (–0.25% per year)	3	42	51	58
High (0.25% per year)	3	38	36	25
Meat or feeds import 10%	3	29	27	20
Investment in research and irrigation				
Low (2% per year)	3	42	70	106
High (4% per year)	3	38	14	–30
World price impact				
Large (0% per year)	3	38	39	37
Small (–1% per year)	3	42	48	48
Salinity and erosion				
Improve (–0.5% per year)	3	35	32	21
Degradation (1.0% per year)	3	45	56	66
Opportunity cost of labour and land				
No change (0% per year)	3	34	28	15
High (2% per year)	3	47	59	71

Source: Huang, Rozelle and Rosegrant, 1995; authors' projections.

short-term tightening of grain supplies, government policy-makers have responded with promises of greater investments in agriculture. While most of these investments have targeted irrigation, improvements in the operations of research institutes have also been announced.

The impacts of China's projected grain trade on the world market are also simulated using IFPRI's IFPTSIM model. The world grain price continues on a declining trend. The results of the simulation show that the magnitude of China's trade will have a strong impact on the trend. If annual net imports of grain were to rise from the 20-30 MMT projected by IFPRI to the 40-43 MMT implied by our baseline projection, the world grain price would decline by about 0.2 per cent annually in 2000-2020. At one extreme, if China were able to achieve grain self-sufficiency, world grain prices could decline by as much as 0.5 per cent per year more than projected by IFPRI in early 2020. On the other hand, if the government is not able to stimulate food production by revising its invest-ment policy, pressing ahead with price and market reform, and improving natural resources, China's net imports of grain could reach about 100 MMT by 2020. This would place further pressure on the world grain market and could even result in there being no decline at all in world grain prices in the early twenty-first century if demand and supply in other countries remained as projected by IFPRI.

V. Concluding remarks

The purpose of this paper was to assess the past performance of China's agriculture and its future supply-demand balance, and then explore the factors that may lie behind past growth and the alternative projections. In the projections of China's future grain demand, supply and trade, the paper's framework includes a demand-side model that accounts not only for the impacts of income and population trends (as well as income response parameters that vary as income levels rise), but also for the effects of urbanisa-tion and the changing level of development of rural consumption markets. The supply response model considers the impact of prices, public investment in research and irriga-tion, institutional change, and environmental factors.

The projections show that under the most plausible expected rates of growth for the important factors, China's imports will rise steadily throughout the next decade. By 2000, imports are expected to reach 40 MMT, a level nearly 3 times higher than their historic peak. Higher imports arise mainly from the accelerating demand for meat and feed grains, as well as from the continued slowing of supply due to reduced investment in agricultural research in the late 1980s. However, after 2000, grain imports are expected to stabilize, as demand growth slows due to increasing urbanisation and declining population growth rates; and supply growth is sustained with the ongoing recovery of investment in agricul-tural research and irrigation.

There is considerable divergence in the projections, however, when baseline assumptions are varied in both the short and long run. Different rates of agricultural investment create some of the largest differences in expected imports, but this is what would be expected from the factor that has the largest marginal output response. While there are a few scenarios where projected levels of imports are somewhat large, both from the viewpoint of China's own domestic needs and relative to the size of current world market trade, there are factors which may keep China from becoming too large a player in the world market. First, world grain prices would certainly rise in the face of large Chinese imports, a tendency which would dampen Chinese grain demand and stimulate domestic supply. Secondly, there may be major foreign exchange constraints to importing such large volumes of grain – either government policy-makers will not allocate foreign exchange for additional grain imports, or exchange rate movements will discourage imports. Thirdly, limitations on the ability of China's ports and other parts of the nation's transportation and marketing infrastructure to handle large quantities of grain may con-strain import levels. Finally, there are many political economy factors that will make China's leaders react to increasing grain shortages. Regardless of China's comparative advantage, government leaders have in the past, and continue to be, concerned with maintaining nearly self-sufficient domestic agricultural production capacity. National defence, pride, and ideology will necessarily put a premium on maintaining a rough balance between domestic demand and supply.

On the basis of the results presented in this paper, it appears that China will neither empty the world grain markets, nor become a major grain exporter. It does seem likely, however, that China will become a more important player in world grain markets as an importer in the coming decades. Both potential exporters outside of China and those charged with managing China's food needs through domestic production and imports need to be ready. Exporting nations – especially those dealing with wheat and maize – will undoubtedly be the beneficiaries of these trends in the short run. If China's policy-makers believe the projected level of imports is too high (either politically or because they see some other physical or economic constraint), investment strategies need to be devised in the near future because of the long lags between the period of expenditure and the time when such investments can affect production. Investment in facilities and institutions needed to handle the increased volume of incoming grain will smooth the shock of production shortfalls, and reduce the time and expense of importing grain. China's foresight in dealing with the upcoming challenge will most likely determine whether the production-demand gap turns into a major agricultural crisis, or whether it will become an opportunity to develop the nation's food economy more effectively.

A framework for forecasting China's grain supply, demand and trade

The major components of this paper's forecasting framework include a supply model for the rice, other grain, and cash cropping sectors of the agricultural economy, and demand models specified separately for rural and urban consumers for rice, grain, meat, and six other animal products. Real-world price projections are generated by IFPTSIM, a partial equilibrium global trade model developed at IFPRI (Rosegrant, Agcaoili-Sombilla and Perez, 1995). In addition to income and prices, the modelling framework for China includes a number of structural and policy variables to account for fundamental forces of transformation in China's rapidly reforming and modernising economy.

Grain production and supply elasticities

The supply model forecasts future trends in China's grain output utilising separate equations for rice and for other grains (total grain minus rice). The parameters used in the supply forecasting model are from Huang, Rosegrant and Rozelle (1995), which are estimated using the normalized quadratic form of the dynamic dual value function approach developed by Epstein (1981). Simultaneously with the two grain supply equations, four other equations – cash crop supply, two quasi-fixed inputs (labour and sown area), and fertilizer – were estimated using a non-linear solution algorithm. Grain output and other explanatory variables are assumed to respond to the crop's own-price, prices of other crops, quasi-fixed and variable inputs, and the off-farm wage. Output also is a function of the stock of agricultural research, the stock of irrigation infrastructure, and three environmental factors: erosion (in the other grain equation), salinisation, and the breakdown of the local environment.[5] The full set of results and detailed discussion of the model can be found in Huang, Rosegrant and Rozelle (1995).

Grain consumption and demand elasticities

Grain consumption is divided into two categories: grain that is directly consumed for food, and that which is fed to animals and consumed indirectly. Direct food equations are divided into rice and other grains. Indirect grain consumption is imputed from the underlying demand equations for pork, beef and mutton, chicken, fish, eggs and milk. The demand equations for all crops are specified separately for rural and urban consumers for all products. Different demand parameters are used for each projection period: the 1990s; 2000-2010; and 2010-2020. Demand is specified as responding to own-price, the price of other major commodities, income, and a variable representing

Annex Table 1.   **Urbanisation and food market development in China, 1990-2020**

	Share of population		Food market development			
			Demand elasticity[a]			
	Rural	Urban	Index[b]	Rice	Other grain	Meat
1990	74	26	45	−0.11	−0.11	0.32
2000	66	34	60	−0.08	−0.08	0.20
2010	58	42	70	−0.06	−0.06	0.10
2020	50	50	80	−0.02	−0.02	0.05

a)   Demand elasticities of rice, other grain, and meat with respect to food market development are a measure of the impact on consumption of the expansion and modernisation of rural food consumption markets, all else remaining constant (*e.g.* income and prices). See Huang and Rozelle (1995*b*) for details.
b)   Food market development index measures the proportion of food bought by rural residents in local food markets. The rest of food is own-produced.
Sources: Population data are from UN. The other data and parameters are from Huang and Rozelle (1995*b*) and Huang and Bouis (1996).

Annex Table 2.   **Assumptions on the growth of factors affecting grain demand in China, 1991-2020**

Factors	Annual growth rate (%)		
	Low	Baseline	High
Total population			
1990-2000	1.142	1.283	1.410
2000-2010	0.491	0.740	0.932
2010-2020	0.374	0.649	0.844
Rural			
1990-2000	0.029	0.158	0.284
2000-2010	−0.844	−0.603	−0.413
2010-2020	−1.030	−0.764	−0.572
Urban			
1990-2000	3.827	3.993	4.124
2000-2010	2.729	2.983	3.180
2010-2020	2.062	2.341	2.539
Per capita real income			
Rural	2.0	3.0	4.0
Urban	2.5	3.5	4.5
Prices			
Rice	0	−0.5	−1.0
Other grain	0	−0.5	−1.0
Meat	−0.5	−0.5	−0.5
Rural market development			
2000	0.60	0.60	0.60
2010	0.70	0.70	0.70
2020	0.80	0.80	0.80

Note: Population estimates are based on UN. Per capita rural income growth figures are similar to those used in World Bank, FAO, and Rosegrant, Agcaoili-Sombilla, and Perez. Output prices are based on simulation analysis performed in collaboration with a model developed by the International Food Policy Research Institute – see Rosegrant, Agcaoili-Sombilla, and Perez. Figures for the rural market development are index numbers for the year indicated (Huang and Rozelle, 1995*b*).

Annex Table 3. **Assumptions on the growth of factors affecting grain supply in China, 1991-2020**

Factors	Annual growth rate (%)		
	Low	Baseline	High
Output and input prices			
Rice	0	−0.5	−1.0
Other grain	0	−0.5	−1.0
Fertilizer	1.0	1.0	1.0
Land and labour			
Land opportunity cost	0	1.0	2.0
Wage	0	1.0	2.0
Agricultural research expenditure	2.0	3.0	4.0
Irrigation expenditure	2.0	3.0	4.0
Environmental factors			
Salinity	−0.5	0.2	1.0
Erosion	−0.5	0.2	1.0

Note: Agricultural research and irrigation expenditures are extrapolated from recent trends and are adjusted based on recent Ministry of Agricultural (MOA) plans (Liu), pronouncements in newspapers, and interviews with MOA and provincial officials. The "land opportunity cost" growth rate is an extrapolation from trends from SPB (1988-92). Land opportunity cost is assumed to be the return to grain cropping (total revenues) net of expenditures for labour (including own labour valued at the market wage), farm chemicals, and other cash expenses. Output price trends are based on simulation analysis performed in collaboration with the IMPACT model developed by the International Food Policy Research Institute – see Rosegrant, Agcaoili-Sombilla, and Perez. Fertilizer price trends are similar to those used by the World Bank. The trends in the deterioration of the environment are based on extrapolations of past trends (Huang and Rozelle, 1994).

the level of development of rural consumption markets (in the rural demand equations). The effect of urbanisation is accounted for by multiplying per capita grain projections for each sector by the projected changes in rural and urban populations, including the anticipated flows of rural residents into the cities.

Income elasticities of demand for rice, other grain, and meat are from Huang and Rozelle (1994), Huang and Rozelle (1995b), and Huang and Bouis (1996). Parameters used to account for the impact of urbanisation and rural food consumption market development are reported in Annex Table 1. All simulations begin from the early 1990s, the base period. Base period data on production and utilisation (discussed above) are three-year averages centred on 1991. Supply-side factors include changes in factor prices, variations in the pattern of government investment in agricultural research and irrigation investment policy, and changes in the state of the environment. Summaries of the assumptions for the major factors affecting future demand and supply growth are in Annex Tables 2 and 3.

Notes

1. Grain in China includes rice, wheat, maize, barley, sorghum, millet, and other coarse grains, as well as soy beans. Potatoes and sweet potatoes are also included but their actual weight is divided by five to turn them into grain equivalents.

2. The urban population has grown from 19 per cent of the total population in 1980 to 28 per cent in 1992, and is expected to reach 50 per cent in 2020.

3. In addition to projected food and feed demand, total grain demand also includes use of grain for seed, nonfood manufacturing, and waste. The projected values of these uses are calculated by maintaining roughly the same ratios as those found in the initial year of the baseline.

4. Import projections are not very sensitive to changes in prices, for two reasons. First, our estimated supply own-price response elasticities are small, a characteristic that is commonly found in other Asian countries where the government frequently intervenes in the agricultural decision-making process. Secondly, on the demand side, although there are fairly large negative own-price elasticities, positive cross-price elasticities dampen the reduction (increase) in demand when prices rise (fall).

5. Technology was measured in stock form, and was built by aggregating past government expenditures on research according to a weighting criteria suggested by Pardey *et al.* (1992). Irrigation stock was constructed by aggregating public expenditures on irrigation, subject to a depreciation rate of 4 per cent per year. The environmental variables have been described and analysed in Huang and Rozelle (1995*a*). The severity of erosion is measured as a ratio of eroded area to cultivated area (which can exceed 1, since eroded area includes both cultivated and non-cultivated areas). Salinisation is the proportion of the total sown area where salinity levels are high enough to affect yields.

Bibliography

BROWN, Lester (1994), "How China Could Starve the World: Its Boom Is Consuming Global Food Supplies", "Outlook" Section, *Washington Post,* 28 August.

CARTER, Colin and Zhong FUNING (1991), "China's Past and Future Role in the Grain Trade", *Economic Development and Cultural Change,* Vol. 39, July, pp. 791-814.

CONROY, Richard (1987), "The Disintegration and Reconstruction of the Rural Science and Technology System" in A. Saith (ed.), *The Reemergence of the Chinese Peasantry,* Croom Helm Press, London.

EPSTEIN, Larry G. (1981), "Duality Theory and Functional Forms for Dynamic Factor Demands", *Review of Economic Studies,* Vol. 48, January, pp. 81-95.

FAN, S. (1991), "Effects of Technological Change and Institutional Reform on Production Growth in Chinese Agriculture", *American Journal of Agricultural Economics,* Vol. 73, pp. 266-275.

FAN, S. and P. PARDEY (1992), *Agricultural Research in China: Its Institutional Development and Impact,* International Service for National Agricultural Research, The Hague.

FAN, S., E.J. WAILES and G.L. CRAMER (1995), "Household Demand in Rural China: A Two-Stage LES-AIDS Model", *American Journal of Agricultural Economics,* Vol. 77, February, pp. 54-62.

FAO [Food and Agricultural Organization] (1991), "Demand Prospects for Rice and Other Food-grains in Selected Asian Countries", Food and Agricultural Organization Economic and Social Development Paper No. 97, Rome.

FINDLAY, Christopher, W. MARTIN and A. WATSEN (1993), *Policy Reform, Economic Growth and China's Agriculture,* OECD, Paris.

HUANG, Jikun and Howath BOUIS (1996), "Structural Changes in the Demand for Food in Asia", Food, Agriculture and the Environment Discussion Paper 11, International Food Policy Research Institute, Washington, DC.

HUANG, Jikun and Cristina C. DAVID (1995), "Policy Reform and Agricultural Incentives in China", Working Paper, International Food Policy Research Institute, Washington, DC.

HUANG, Jikun, Mark ROSEGRANT and Scott ROZELLE (1995), "Public Investment, Techno-logical Change and Agricultural Growth in China", Paper presented at the Final Conference on the Medium- and Long-Term Projections of World Rice Supply and Demand, sponsored by the International Food Policy Research Institute and the International Rice Research Institute, Beijing, 23-26 April.

HUANG, Jikun and Scott ROZELLE (1994), "Income, Quality, and the Demand for Food in Rural China", Working Paper, Food Research Institute, Stanford University.

91

HUANG, Jikun and Scott ROZELLE (1995a), "Environmental Stress and Grain Yields in China", *American Journal of Agricultural Economics,* Vol. 77, November, pp. 853-864.

HUANG, Jikun and Scott ROZELLE (1995b), "Market Development and Food Demand in Rural China", FCND Discussion Paper No. 5, International Food Policy Research Institute, Washington, DC.

HUANG, Jikun and Scott ROZELLE (forthcoming), "Technological Change: Rediscovering the Engine of Productivity Growth in China's Agricultural Economy", *Journal of Development Economics.*

HUANG, Jikun, Scott ROZELLE and Mark ROSEGRANT (1995), "China's Food Economy to the 21st Century: Supply, Demand and Trade", IFPRI's 2020 Discussion Paper, International Food Policy Research Institute, Washington, DC.

LARDY, N. (1983), *Agriculture in China's Modern Economic Development,* Cambridge University Press, Cambridge.

LIN, Justin Yifu (1988), "The Household Responsibility System in China's Agricultural Reform: A Theoretical and Empirical Study", *Economic Development and Cultural Change,* Vol. 36 (Supplement), April.

LIN, Justin Yifu (1991), "The Household Responsibility System Reform and the Adoption of Hybrid Rice in China", *Journal of Development Economics,* Vol. 36, pp. 353-373.

LIN, Justin Yifu (1992), "Rural Reforms and Agricultural Growth in China", *American Economic Review,* Vol. 82, pp. 34-51.

LIN, Justin Yifu (1994), "Rural Reforms and Policy Changes in China's Grain Economy", prepared for the Third Workshop on Projections and Policy Implications of Medium- and Long-Term Rice Supply Demand, the International Rice Research Institute and the International Food Policy Research Institute, Bangkok, 24-26 January.

McMILLAN, John, John WHALLEY and Lijing ZHU (1989), "The Impact of China's Economic Reforms on Agricultural Productivity Growth", *Journal of Political Economy,* Vol. 97, pp. 781-807.

MEI, Fangquan (1995), "China Can Feed Its Population", *China Daily,* 29 April.

NICKUM, James E. (1982), "Irrigation Management in China: A Review of the Literature", World Bank Staff Working Paper 545, World Bank, Washington, DC.

PARDEY, Phil, R. LINDNER, E. ABDURACHMAN, S. WOOD, S. FAN, W. EVELEENS, B. ZHANG and J. ALSTON (1992), "The Economic Returns to Indonesian Rice and Soybean Research", Report prepared by the Agency for Agricultural Research and Development (AARD) and the International Service for National Agricultural Research (ISNAR), November.

PERKINS D. and S. YUSUF (1984), *Rural Development in China,* The Johns Hopkins University Press, Baltimore, Maryland.

PRAY, Carl, Scott ROZELLE and Jikun HUANG (1995), "Agricultural Research in China: Growth and Reforms", Working Paper, Department of Agricultural Economics, Rutgers University.

ROSEGRANT, Mark, Mercedita AGCAOILI-SOMBILLA and Nicostrato PEREZ (1995), "Rice and the Global Food Economy: Projections and Policy Implications of Future Food Balances", Paper presented at the Final Conference on the Medium- and Long-Term Projections of World Rice Supply and Demand, sponsored by the International Food Policy Research Institute and the International Rice Research Institute, Beijing, 23-26 April.

ROZELLE, Scott, Albert PARK and Jikun HUANG (1995), "Dilemmas in Reforming State-Market Relations in Rural China", Working Paper, Food Research Institute, Stanford University.

ROZELLE, Scott, Jikun HUANG and Gregory VEECK (forthcoming), "The Impact of Environmental Degradation on Grain Production in China", *Economic Geography.*

SICULAR, Terry (1995), "China's Agricultural Policy During the Reform Period" in M.E. Sharpe (ed.), *China's Economic Dilemmas in the 1990s: The Problems of Reforms, Modernization, and Interdependence,* Joint Economic Committee, Congress of the United States, Armonk, New York, pp. 340-364.

STONE, Bruce (1988), "Developments in Agricultural Technology", *China Quarterly,* Vol. 116, December.

TANG, Anthony (1984), *An Analytical and Empirical Investigation of Agriculture in Mainland China, 1952-80,* Chung-hwa Institute of Economic Research, Chinese Taipei.

UNITED NATIONS (1993), "World Population Prospects: 1992 Revisions", Report from the United Nations Department of Economic, Social Information, and Policy Analysis, New York.

WEINS, T. (1982), "The Limits to Agricultural Intensification: The Suzhou Experience", *China under the Four Modernization, Part I,* US Government Printing Office, pp. 462-474.

WEN, J.G. (1993), "Total Factor Productivity Change In China's Farming Sector: 1952-89", *Economic Development and Cultural Change,* Vol. 42, pp. 1-42.

WORLD BANK (1990), *Agriculture to the Year 2000: A World Bank Country Study (Annex 2 to China: Long-term Development Issues and Options),* Washington, DC.

ZGTJNJ (1980-93), *Zhongguo Tongji Nianjian* [China Statistical Yearbook], China Statistical Press, Beijing.

In Chinese

CAAS [Chinese Academy of Agricultural Sciences] (1985), Abstract of the Comprehensive Report on "Study of the Development of Grain and Cash Crops Production in China", *Study of the Development of Grain and Cash Crop Development in China,* Volume 4, Beijing.

LIN, Justin Yifu (1995), "A Study of Grain Yield Potential and Research Priority", *Zhongguo Nonch Guancha* [China Rural Observation], No. 2, March.

LIU, Jiang (1991), *Quanguo nongcun jingji fazhan: Shinian guihua he dibage wunian jihua* [Rural Economic Development of China: Ten-Year Plan and the Eighth Five-Year Plan], Ministry of Agriculture Press, Beijing.

SPB [State Price Bureau] (1988-92), *Quanguo nongchanpin chengben shouyi ziliao huibian* [National Agricultural Production Cost and Revenue Information Summary], China Price Bureau Press, Beijing.

SSTC [State Science and Technology Commission], *Zhongguo Kexue Jishu Ziliao Ku, 1985-90;* 1993 [China Science and Technology Statistical Yearbook, 1985-90; 1993].

China's Long-term Energy Outlook[1]

by

Robert Priddle
Executive Director
International Energy Agency, OECD

I. Introduction

There are many reasons for China's growing importance in world economic, energy and environmental affairs. With a population of close to 1.2 billion, China is the most populous country in the world. If the size of its economy is measured using United Nations estimates of purchasing power parities, China is already the second largest economy in the world.[2] China has become one of the largest trading nations, and it is likely to be progressively more important if its economy continues to expand at or near recent rates of growth. China's foreign trade performance in 1994 was impressive. It turned a $12 billion trade deficit in 1993 into a surplus of over $5 billion. This pattern of expanding trade will lead to an increasing influence both on the Pacific region and on the world economy. Also, since China already accounts for more than a tenth of world carbon emissions, the manner of dealing with its growing energy needs will be critical for its own and the world's environment over the next two decades and beyond.

China is equally important from an analytical point of view. Its economic perform-ance over the past fifteen years has been very impressive, not only because of the fast economic growth achieved but also because of the relatively modest growth in its energy needs. Between 1983 and 1993, China's energy demand grew at around 5 per cent per annum, significantly less than the economic growth rate of over 9 per cent. Such a decline in energy intensity is an achievement rarely seen in countries at the level of development of China. In the context of the environmental debate of recent years, where protection of the environment often appears to contradict the growth objectives of developing coun-tries, it is important to understand the reasons for China's performance and to determine whether there are lessons for other countries. This issue is briefly discussed at the end of the chapter.

In order to maintain its rate of economic growth, China must be able either to produce or import the necessary energy that a rapid economic expansion has historically required, or to find new ways of developing with lower energy intensities. Energy is likely to remain a very important factor for China's development, and there are already many reports that energy shortages are becoming a hindrance to growth. According to a 1991 study from the Asian Development Bank, electricity supply for township and village industries satisfied only 40 per cent of the potential demand, while most of the oil-intensive agricultural machinery could only work for 160 hours per year (Asian Development Bank, 1991, p. 239). Other reports indicate that up to a quarter of Chinese industry may frequently be forced to be idle due to power shortages. Shortages are not limited to energy and often affect many other basic materials such as steel and cement. In fact, imports are often relied on to cover important industrial needs.

Significance of China in the world energy market

The high level of energy consumption and production makes China one of the major forces in world energy markets. Developments in the Chinese energy market can have far-reaching effects in world energy trade and prices. Therefore, national energy policies and the evolution of energy demand/supply patterns are of significant importance for other countries and regions.

In 1993 China was the third-largest energy producer in the world after the United States and Russia. For example, China's coal production (over 1 150 million tonnes) accounts for about one-third of the world's total coal supply. Similarly, with a current production level of approximately 3 million barrels per day, China is one of the major oil-producing countries. On the other hand, China's share in total world energy demand is large and expected to become larger still. As shown in Table 1, the Chinese economy currently consumes about 9 per cent of world total energy demand. It is expected that this share will increase significantly and rise close to 13 per cent by 2010, due to a higher rate of growth in demand than the rest of the world. The current quarter share of total world coal consumption is also expected to grow and reach close to one-third by 2010. Similarly, high demand for electricity is expected to result in a share of about 11 per cent in world total electricity output in 2010. It is also expected that the projected modest increase in oil production compared with that of demand could make China a major oil importer with a significant impact on world oil trade.

Table 1.   **China's share in world energy demand (%)**

	1971	1993	2000	2010
Solids	12.6	23.9	27.9	31.1
Oil	1.7	4.3	5.7	7.4
Electricity gen.	2.6	6.2	8.5	10.7
Total primary energy demand	4.9	8.9	10.9	12.7

Source: IEA.

Figure 1a. **China's carbon dioxide emissions**

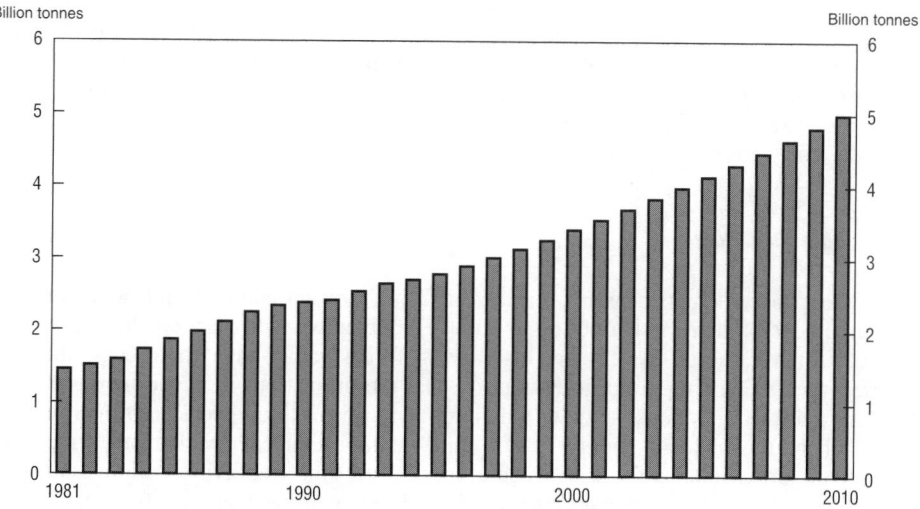

Billion tonnes

Source: IEA.

Figure 1b. **Increase in annual carbon dioxide emissions, 1990-2010**

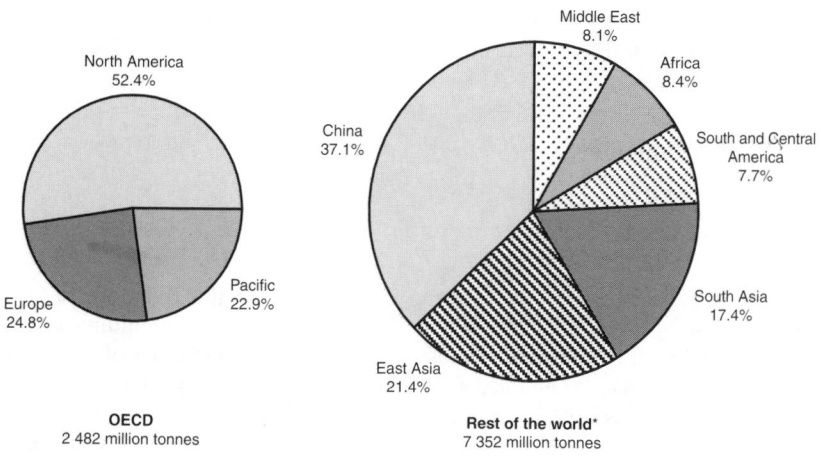

OECD
2 482 million tonnes

Rest of the world*
7 352 million tonnes

* World excluding the OECD, the former Soviet Union and Eastern Europe.
Source: IEA.

In parallel to its significance in the world energy market, China's current carbon dioxide emissions account for a significant proportion of world carbon dioxide emissions. China's emissions in 1993 accounted for 12.6 per cent of world carbon dioxide emissions, as compared with 5 per cent in 1971. As illustrated in Figures 1a and 1b, the contribution of China to global carbon emissions is expected to increase substantially, mainly due to extensive use of coal. It is projected that China's share in world carbon dioxide emissions will account for almost 17 per cent by 2010.

Methodological note

This paper attempts a brief overview of China's recent energy trends and examines potential developments in the period to 2010. The objective is to increase the understanding of China's energy system and its driving forces rather than to forecast the next fourteen years. It is important to emphasize that the projections included here are based on very many assumptions, some of which are built on relatively weak information. Data on much of the Chinese energy system and on important energy demand drivers are scarce, or are available for a very short period of time, rendering serious statistical analysis difficult. Such data weaknesses include standardized energy balances before 1980, end-use energy prices, much of standard macroeconomic data prior to 1978 and figures for non-commercial energy use.

Even without data problems, the dramatic changes in the Chinese economy and energy system over the past fifteen years would make any standard techniques of extrapolation of previous trends highly dubious as a method of deriving projections for China.[3] Policy mechanisms and behaviour by economic agents, two of the most important constants in standard econometric analysis, are in the process of substantial change. Thus, the model underlying the projections presented here is primarily a logical framework, within which the energy consequences of the assumed economic activity levels and efficiency trends can be derived in a consistent fashion.

II. Major assumptions

Economic growth

China has been a rapidly growing economy since the founding of the People's Republic, although until the 1960s it was still primarily an agriculture-based economy despite the political emphasis on industry. The overall growth rate of the economy, and especially of industry, accelerated following the reforms of the late 1970s, and annual growth since 1980 has been over 9 per cent. Due to the previous structure of the economy and to the nature of policy reform, the fast economic growth in recent years has not affected all regions and sectors equally. For example, while the overall growth rate in 1994 was a very impressive 11.8 per cent, agricultural output grew at only about 3.5 per cent compared with 18 per cent growth in the industrial sector. Similarly, there was a big gap between the growth rate in the state-owned sector, which grew at 8.5 per cent, and the collective and private sectors, which grew at 22 and 31 per cent, respectively.

In the recently drafted Ninth Five-Year Plan (1996-2000), the Chinese economy is expected to grow at rates similar to those of the first half of 1990s, with the goal of becoming the world's third-largest economy (after the United States and Japan).[4] The plan foresees China evolving into a major force among Asian countries, attracting extensive amounts of foreign capital and establishing its own multinational companies. On the other hand, it is also underlined in the new five-year plan that the increasing need for petroleum imports could create bottlenecks and balance-of-payments difficulties.

Table 2. **GDP growth rates in China**

% p.a.

	1983 to 1993	1993 to 2000	2000 to 2010
China	9.4	8.5	7.0

Source: ZGTJNJ, 1994; IEA assumptions.

In this study, the economy is projected to grow by 10 per cent in 1995, around 8 per cent in the rest of the 1990s, and by 7 per cent in the following decade. The assumed growth rates for China are higher than those assumed in other developing countries in the region; they are similar to GDP growth rates achieved in South Korea in the 1980s. It is assumed here that policy reform will continue in China and that the world economy, on which China will become increasingly dependent, will not hinder its growth prospects.

There are many difficulties that must be overcome for China to continue on its current rapid growth path. These include political uncertainties, since it is not clear that all social groupings receive sufficient attention within China's current political system. Also, the current difficulties in dealing with the overheating of the economy indicate that future rapid growth may well require a strong central authority that is in a position to co-ordinate effective macroeconomic policy. Such authority may be difficult to establish given China's tradition of regional economic autonomy and the further decentralisation which has been part of the successful reforms of the past fifteen years. Finally, the difficulties involved in transforming the large state enterprises, and the severe bottlenecks in many vital sectors of the economy, including energy and transportation, may well hinder future growth.

Economic structure[5]

One of the key features of the Chinese economy is the very large share of industry in the overall economy, given China's apparent stage of development. As shown in Table 3, the current share of industry in total GDP is about 48 per cent, compared to 27 and 43 per cent for India and Korea, respectively. The contribution of industry to the overall

Table 3. **Shares in gross domestic product (%)**

	1978	1993	2000	2010
Agriculture	28.4	22.5	20	16
Industry	48.6	48.5	44	42
Services	23.0	29.0	36	42

Source: 1978 and 1993 based on ZGTJNJ, 1994; others from IEA assumptions.

economy in other low-income countries varies between 10 and 25 per cent, while that of upper-middle-income countries is on average 40 per cent, both significantly lower than the share of industry in the Chinese economy (World Bank, 1995). The share of agriculture in total GDP is lower than industry's, and it decreased from 28.4 per cent in 1978 to 22.5 per cent in 1993.

In this study, it is assumed that the share of agriculture will gradually decline to 20 per cent by 2000 and 16 per cent by 2010. Industry is assumed to grow slightly more slowly than the overall economy, and its share declines modestly over the outlook period. The service sector is assumed to continue to expand much faster than the overall economy, and its share approaches that of industry by 2010. These changes in the overall structure are quite sharp even for a period of twenty years, but they are feasible during a period of very fast economic growth.[6]

Population assumptions

It is assumed that China will be successful in limiting the growth in population to slightly over 1 per cent per annum during the 1990s and to less than 0.7 per cent towards the end of the projection period. This compares with an OECD average population growth rate of 0.3 per cent from 2000 to 2010. Even with a slightly lower growth rate over the second half of the outlook period, China's population will be very close to 1.4 billion by 2010. It should be noted that the success of the one child policy may be put at risk if, as the country develops, the ability of central authority to influence individuals erodes and more children are seen as a sign of wealth by families who can afford the financial penalties involved. From an energy point of view, the likely trend in urbanisation is as important as overall population growth. The current urban population is around 330 million, or around 28 per cent of the total population. The urban share in total population is expected to rise to 40 per cent or to just over 550 million people by 2010, though it is possible that even this increase could prove an underestimate.

Power generation assumptions

Hydro and renewables

China has a vast potential for hydro power generation; according to official figures, this potential amounts to 676 GW, out of which 379 GW is suitable for exploitation

(People's Republic of China Yearbook, 1990). However, most of this capacity is quite far from populated areas and industrial centres. The current available capacity, at around 43 GW, represents about 10 per cent of the potential. A very large proportion of current hydro plants are very small-scale. According to the Asian Development Bank, around 60 per cent of the 2 000 counties in China have their own mini hydro schemes, and more than half of these counties rely on hydro for their electricity. The variable flows of many of these small plants lead to the relatively low aggregate capacity factor of under 40 per cent. The capacity factor is projected to increase to 45 per cent, as many of the new schemes will be on a larger scale than many of the existing plants. Hydro power makes up around a third of the 60 GW of electricity-generating plants currently under construction in China. The controversial Three Gorges River project has been approved although the financial arrangements have not been finalised. With a capacity of more than 17 GW, the Three Gorges project could make a very significant contribution to China's electricity needs. The project, however, has a very high cost and it is not clear whether it will be completed before 2010 as planned. Hydro capacity is projected to grow to just over 70 GW by 2000 and to 123 GW by 2010. These projections are somewhat lower than the revised official plans, which now project close to 80 GW of hydro capacity by 2000.

There is a small amount of wind-power generation in China, around 15 MW in 1992, and official plans project an increase to 1 GW by 2000. This is likely to prove optimistic due to the high cost of the mostly imported technology.

Nuclear

China currently has 2.3 GW of nuclear capacity in two nuclear plants: a small 300 MW reactor at Qinshan in Eastern Zhejiang and two PWR reactors at Daya Bay rated at 984 MW each.

Official plans for 2000, at least until recently, aimed to have 6 GW of available capacity and 6 GW under construction by that date, and to bring on 1.2 GW per year after 2000. These targets seem very optimistic – especially for the period to 2000 – given the long period of construction required for nuclear plants. The projected gross capacity by the year 2000 is put at 2.3 GW, as only Daya 1 and Daya 2 are assumed to be operational by that date. Three more units at Qingshan in Zhejiang Province are then projected to bring capacity to 3.7 GW by 2003 and a further 1 GW is added annually beyond that for a total nuclear capacity of 10.6 GW by 2010. Under an optimistic nuclear scenario, the installed capacity by 2000 could be up to 3.7 GW and then grow by the official target of 1.2 GW per year to reach 15.7 GW by 2010. The capacity factor has been assumed to be 74 per cent throughout the outlook period.

III. Energy demand

Introduction

Key features and recent developments

China is the third-largest energy-consuming country in the world behind the United States and Russia. Perhaps the most outstanding feature of the Chinese energy system is its extreme dependence on coal which, in 1993, accounted for more than three-quarters of primary energy and more than two-thirds of final commercial energy consumed.[7] Oil accounted for about 20 per cent of the remaining primary energy consumption, with gas and hydro sharing the very small residual. Primary gas consumption in China is insignificant and used mostly for production of chemicals and fertilizers. The share of electricity in final consumption, at about 10 per cent, is very small. Direct heat output, which is grouped together with electricity in this outlook, accounted for a further 3 per cent of final energy consumption in 1993. Nearly three-quarters of electricity generation is from coal-fired plants, with the bulk of the remainder coming from hydroelectricity.

Industrial energy consumption accounted for almost 60 per cent of China's final commercial energy consumption in 1993, a proportion much higher than in many other countries at the same level of development. While the exclusion of non-commercial energy tends to exaggerate the proportion of industrial energy use, several factors – including policy initiatives prior to 1990 which emphasized the development of heavy industry – have contributed to the evolution of many energy-intensive industries. Indeed, the iron and steel and chemical sectors each account for nearly a quarter of total energy consumption in the industrial sector, with the non-metallic minerals and building materials (e.g. cement) sectors consuming a further 17 per cent. In contrast with industry, transportation accounts for a very small proportion of final energy consumption, about 10 per cent in 1993. Coal still plays an important role in the transportation sector, where coal-fired steam locomotives account for a very large proportion of rail transportation.

Residential and commercial sector energy consumption accounts for just over 20 per cent of final consumption. This is to some extent due to the lack of commercial fuels in the rural areas, where the bulk of the population lives. It is estimated that 75 per cent of domestic rural energy consumption is biomass.

From 1983 to 1993, primary and final energy consumption grew at an annual rate slightly higher than 5 per cent. Over the same period, final oil consumption grew by about 6.4 per cent, solids consumption by 3.4 per cent, gas by 6.5 per cent and electricity consumption by about 9 per cent. In 1993 growth in demand for electricity and oil products was especially strong at nearly 9 and 10 per cent, respectively. These growth trends have accentuated the problems of energy shortages, especially in China's fastest-growing areas.

Summary outlook

Over the outlook period, primary energy demand in China is expected to grow at 4 per cent per annum. Solids demand is projected to grow at 3.4 per cent per annum, oil demand at around 5 per cent and gas at 8 per cent. By 2010, the share of solids in primary energy demand is expected to fall slightly below 70 per cent while the share of oil will rise to 22 per cent. Gas will remain marginal, with its share expected to remain below 4 per cent. Nuclear is expected to increase its post-2000 share to over 1 per cent, while the share of hydro in primary demand is limited to 3 per cent over the outlook period.

The share of coal in final consumption over the outlook period is expected to exhibit an even more dramatic decline, from 64 per cent in 1993 to just over 53 per cent in 2010,

Figure 2. **Final energy demand by fuel**

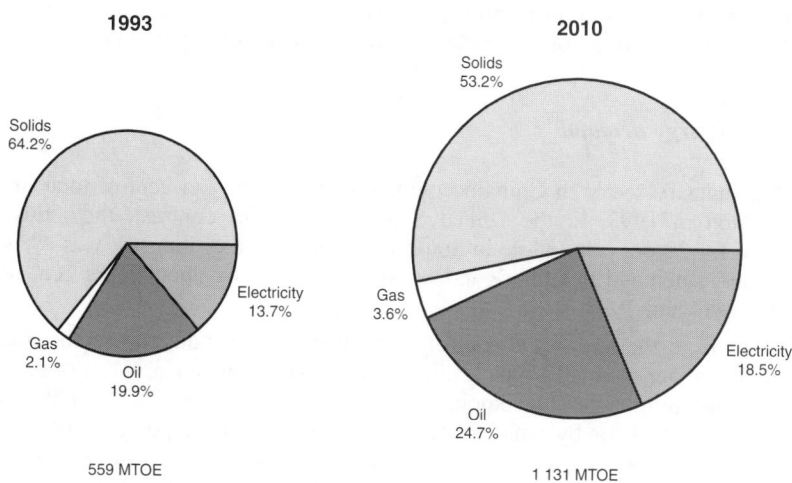

1993

559 MTOE

2010

1 131 MTOE

Source: IEA.

Figure 3. **Final energy demand by sector**

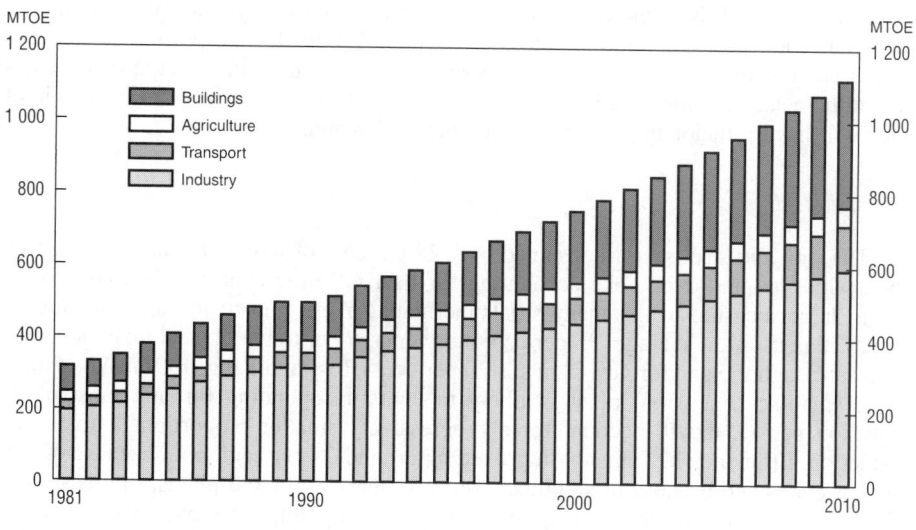

Source: IEA.

than the coal share in primary energy demand. Oil and electricity will both increase their share, to around 25 per cent and 19 per cent, respectively. Growth in final consumption for both of these fuels, at close to 6 per cent per annum, will be over twice as rapid as growth in coal consumption, projected to grow at 3 per cent per annum.

Industrial energy demand

The industry sector in China accounted for almost 60 per cent of total final energy consumption in 1993. In the United States, by way of contrast, the industry sector accounted for 29 per cent, while in South Korea the share of industry was 49 per cent in 1993. Energy demand in China's industrial sector grew by about 5 per cent per annum between 1983 and 1993.

Apart from the large state-controlled companies, the industrial sector consists of a very large number of small firms, leading to an almost complete absence of economies of scale. According to Asian Development Bank estimates, 52 per cent of industrial value-added is accounted for by small-scale enterprises. Excluding power generation boilers and railway locomotives, there are some 200 000 industrial boilers consuming about 140 million tonnes of oil equivalent with only 50 per cent efficiency, compared with 70 to 80 per cent internationally (Asian Development Bank, 1993). A major reason for this efficiency gap is the common small scale of most of the boilers in China. A large portion of Chinese industry is expected to continue to be on a relatively small scale over the outlook period, due to the increasing importance of rural enterprises. These now account for around 30 per cent of total enterprises, and their share is likely to rise to 40 per cent by 2000.

Nearly two-thirds of industrial energy consumption currently takes place in the iron and steel, chemical and building material sectors. While this proportion is likely to decline significantly over the projection period, it is important, in the case of China, to look at these sectors individually, as trends in the underlying industries and their technologies will have a major impact on overall energy demand.

Iron and steel

The iron and steel sector consumed over 28 per cent of industrial energy demand in 1991, with coal and oven coke accounting for nearly 90 per cent of this consumption. Due in large measure to the many small inefficient plants and to the unavailability of scrap, China uses, on average, 35 per cent more energy per tonne of steel than the United States, although the gap for new plants is 20 per cent (Ross and Feng, 1991). While much of the small-scale and old plant is likely to continue operating through most of the projection period, it will account for a progressively smaller proportion of total steel production. Efficiency has already improved by around 20 per cent, both because of new efficient plants and because of significant retro-fitting of some old plants. In this study it has been assumed that the intensity of existing capacity improves by 0.5 per cent per annum, while all post-1990 capacity is 35 per cent less energy-intensive than the 1990 average level.

China appears to be one of the most steel-intensive countries in the world, although – as with energy intensities – international comparisons are subject to severe interpretation and measurement problems. Chinese steel consumption rose by 7.7 per cent per annum between 1970 and 1993. Immense infrastructural needs, as well as the expected rapid growth in the construction and other steel-intensive industries, will lead to continued growth in steel consumption (projected at around 2.5 per cent per annum from 1993 to 2010).

China's steel production expanded from 37 million tonnes in 1980 to 90 million tonnes in 1993, with capacity utilisation at almost 100 per cent in recent years. Production is projected to increase by around 3.5 per cent per annum, and to approach 160 million tonnes by 2010. Despite this high rate of domestic growth, China is likely to remain a major importer of steel; its imports are expected to amount to around 10 to 20 per cent of its consumption through most of the period. One of the reasons for continued steel import dependency could be the relative shortage of iron ore in China.

Overall energy demand in the iron and steel sector is projected to grow by about 2 per cent over the outlook period. There is no projected use of minimills due to the country's lack of scrap. Hence the iron and steel industry is expected to continue to be dominated by coal.

Chemicals

Energy consumption in the chemical industry accounts for just under a quarter of total industrial energy demand. As with many other sectors, the use of coal as a feedstock in small-scale plants leads to very large inefficiencies. Even within China, small coal-based plants are twice as energy-intensive as large-scale gas-based plants. Despite this, small coal plants have grown especially rapidly over the past fifteen years. The chemical sector is dominated by the fertilizer industry, with a large proportion of this industry producing ammonia. The use of commercial fertilizers is likely to grow faster than agricultural output due to the increasing use of marginal land, land shortages and the increasing requirements for higher agricultural production. As energy demand in the rural residential sector shifts toward commercial fuels, however, the use of crop residue and organic chemicals for agricultural purposes may dampen the expected increase in fertilizer demand.

Production of basic chemicals, while representing a small proportion of the total chemical sector in China, is expected to grow especially rapidly over the outlook period. (For a discussion of this sector see Vergara and Babelon, 1990.) There are severe shortages of basic chemicals and, despite a projected near-doubling in the production of ethylene to 5 million tonnes by 2000, China is likely to remain a major importer of these products. Ethylene production could double again by 2010, to 10 million tonnes. The overall energy demand in the chemical sector is projected to increase by 3.1 per cent per annum between 1993 and 2010, compared with a corresponding rate of growth in chemical output of just under 5 per cent.

Cement

Production of building materials including, in particular, cement is hampered by chronic shortages and by the large proportion of production coming from small plants with no economies of scale and often antiquated technologies. According to some estimates, the average energy consumption per tonne of cement produced was 50 per cent higher than in modern plants. Moreover, only 18 per cent of production originated from medium- and large-scale plants (World Bank, 1993). Cement demand is expected to be driven both by a building boom in the residential and commercial sectors and by large infrastructural and industrial construction projects. Despite the quadrupling of cement production over the past fifteen years, its growth has been projected at a more modest 60 per cent of the GDP growth rate on the basis of assumed improvements in building technology. Cement production is expected to reach around 670 million tonnes by 2010. Scarcity of funds and the need for increases in capacity are likely to prevent replacement of much of the current cement production capacity, and the average efficiency improvement has been assumed to be limited to 1 per cent per annum. Thus, energy demand in the building materials sector is expected to increase by about 4 per cent per annum over the projection period.

Other industry

The remainder of Chinese industry is expected to be characterised by falling energy intensities as it continues to move to high-value-added products. Based on statistical estimation, the energy demand in this sector is expected to grow by only a quarter of the rate of growth of overall industrial production. However, given the fast economic growth rate and the even faster growth in non-energy-intensive industry, energy demand is still expected to grow by nearly 80 per cent from its 1993 level. The shift in fuel shares away from coal toward electricity will be particularly noticeable in this sector, with coal's share falling to under 60 per cent and electricity's rising to close to 30 per cent.

Total industry demand projections

The share of industrial energy demand in total final energy demand is projected to fall to just over 50 per cent in 2010. This decline reflects the small drop in the share of industry in GDP as well as the transport sector's increasing share of final energy demand. The level of industrial energy demand is expected to grow by 3 per cent over the outlook period – which, given that industrial output is projected to grow by around 8 per cent, implies further declines in industrial energy intensity.

Electricity is expected to be substituted for coal in many industries, leading to an increase in electricity's share from around 17 to over 22 per cent and a decline in solids' share from 69 to 63 per cent over the outlook period.

Residential and commercial energy demand

Residential and commercial energy demand grew at close to 4 per cent per annum from 1983 to 1993. As in most other sectors in China, coal is the dominant fuel, with

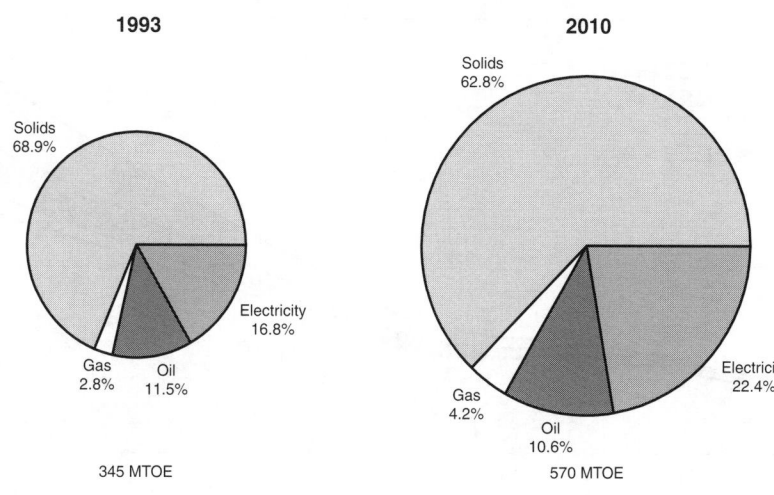

Figure 4. **Industrial energy demand by share of fuel**

1993

Solids
68.9%

Electricity
16.8%

Gas
2.8%

Oil
11.5%

345 MTOE

2010

Solids
62.8%

Electricity
22.4%

Gas
4.2%

Oil
10.6%

570 MTOE

Source: IEA.

slightly less than an 80 per cent share in 1993. Electricity consumption, however, grew very rapidly over the period, at about 13 per cent per annum, due to the sharp increase in the penetration of appliances and the electrification of rural areas. The overall future trends in residential and commercial energy demand will depend on four factors: first, on the rate at which commercial fuels are substituted for non-commercial fuels, especially in rural areas; secondly, on the increase in building space for both residential and commercial purposes; thirdly, on the rate of increase of purchases of new appliances, which

Table 4. **Industrial energy demand**

Mtoe

	1983	1993	2000	2010
Solids	161	238	288	358
Oil	22	40	48	61
Gas	6	10	14	24
Electricity	26	58	83	128
Total	214	345	433	570

Source: IEA.

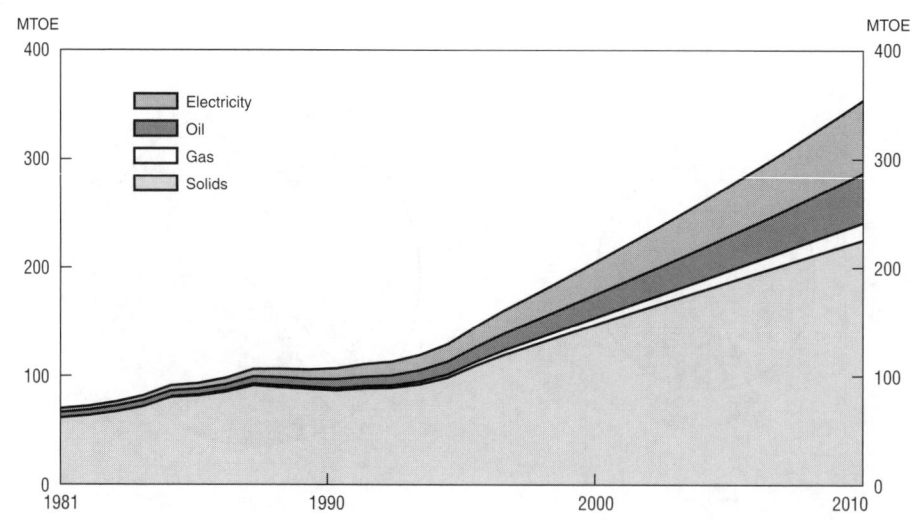

Figure 5. **Residential and commercial energy demand**

Source: IEA.

depends to a large extent on growth in household income; and finally, on efficiency trends in construction and appliances.

The cumulative result of these factors is a threefold increase in the projected commercial energy demand in the residential and commercial sectors, from 113 million tonnes of oil equivalent in 1993 to around 350 million tonnes by 2010. The implied growth rate of close to 7 per cent per annum is significantly below that of GDP despite the fact that commercial energy demand growth takes account of the assumed reduction in availability of non-commercial energy. The growth rate of total energy used in the sector, *i.e.* including non-commercial energy, is less than 3 per cent. Thus, the ability of non-commercial fuels – which still amount to close to 120 Mtoe by 2010 – to satisfy even the 25 per cent share assumed here is one of the major uncertainties in this sector. Growth of energy demand in the sector is assumed to be supply-constrained until 1995. Similarly, if the sector as a whole were to grow in line with the GDP projections, the demand for commercial energy by 2010 would exceed 1 billion tonnes of oil equivalent, even with no decline in the level of non-commercial energy available. While such a number is clearly unrealistic, it indicates the scope of uncertainty in the projections presented here.

While coal is projected to remain the dominant fuel in the sector, its share is likely to decline significantly. Partly for environmental reasons, official policy strongly encourages the growth of gas in residential areas. Gas networks already exist in many cities,

Table 5. **Residential and commercial energy demand**

Mtoe

	1983	1993	2000	2010
Solids	67.1	89.0	144.5	225.1
Oil	4.7	9.0	20.5	45.6
Gas	0.7	2.3	5.2	16.1
Electricity	3.8	12.6	29.0	67.2
Total	76.3	113.0	200.2	354.0

Source: IEA.

although much of the gas used is derived from coal. Given the potential for rapid urbanisation and for growth in new construction, the increase in the share of gas in the residential/commercial sector could be potentially very large over the outlook period. In the projections, the share of solids declines from 79 to 64 per cent of total commercial energy while the share of gas more than doubles to nearly 5 per cent. The growth in electricity is expected to be very fast, especially in the commercial sector; its share doubles to 19 per cent by 2010.

The commercial sector, in particular, has immense scope for further development in China and is likely to grow very sharply over the projection period. Per capita electricity consumption in this sector in 1989 amounted to 24 kWh/year, compared with 265 in Brazil, 387 in Korea and nearly 3 000 in the United States (Feng, 1993). It is unlikely that the building boom in most city centres will end before 2010, as long as a positive economic climate prevails. The projections of energy demand in the commercial sector are based on an estimated income elasticity of 0.9.

Transportation energy demand

China's overall transportation energy demand is very low, both in absolute terms and in comparison with the total amount of energy used in the country.[8] For example, in 1993, the proportion of final energy used in transportation was 33 per cent of total final energy demand in OECD countries and 23 per cent in developing countries as a whole, but only 10 per cent in China. Future trends in transportation energy demand will clearly depend on both increasing needs with regard to moving goods and people, and the extent to which the efficiency of transportation equipment will improve.

Road transportation

According to official statistics, total passenger kilometres driven in China grew by an average of over 10 per cent per annum in the period 1979-93. Total passenger kilometres in 1993 were 785 billion, nearly 40 per cent higher than in 1990 but still corresponding to under 700 kilometres per person per year. This compares with over 13 000 kilometres per person in the United States. From 1979 to 1993, passenger railway use grew by almost 8 per cent while highway passenger kilometres grew by just under 14 per cent per annum. The increasing penetration of road travel is quite consistent both with the general trend in growing economies toward more independent travel, and with the specific trend in China of increasing pressure on the railway system from freight transportation. Thus, passenger kilometres by road are expected to grow significantly faster than overall travel; the share is likely to be around 55 per cent by 2010, compared with 47 per cent in 1993 and 32 per cent in 1980.

These growth rates in passenger road usage are quite in line with growth rates in the number of vehicles. For example, the number of small cars grew from less than 250 000 in 1980 to almost 1.3 million vehicles in 1990. Over the same period, the number of buses tripled and the number of motorcycles grew by 17 times. In 1993, the number of small cars is estimated to have been close to 2 million, and it is expected to approach 4 million by 2000. Even such dramatic growth will leave Chinese ownership of cars at less than one car per 250 persons.

Efficiency trends in passenger transportation will be determined by two contradic-tory trends that are likely to develop. On the one hand, as in any other region, technologi-cal improvements may lead to more efficient vehicles over the next twenty years. The relatively small number of vehicles currently in China, compared with the likely number by 2010, means that the average efficiency in the future is likely to be much higher than that of today. This is indeed already apparent, as gasoline and diesel use per 100 vehicle kilometres has fallen from 30 and 26.9 litres in 1985 to 27.7 and 23.1, respectively, in 1992. On the other hand, there is a likelihood – supported by the trends between 1985 and 1993 – that with growing personal incomes, people will shift gradually to more individual and comfortable means of transport (*i.e.* cars rather than buses, motorcycles rather than bicycles, and less overcrowded public means of transport). Despite the above improvements in efficiency per vehicle kilometre, the efficiency per 100 passenger kilometres (which takes into account the persons-per-vehicle density) has actually deteri-orated by more than 10 per cent for both diesel- and gasoline-driven vehicles (from 8 and 6.1 litres to 9.1 and 7 litres, respectively).

It is difficult to estimate which of the two factors influencing vehicle efficiency is likely to prove more significant over the projection period. Given the immense scope for more private and comfortable travel in China, it has nevertheless been assumed, some-what optimistically, that the efficiency per passenger kilometre improves by 1 per cent per year.

Freight transportation, in tonne kilometres, has grown at roughly the same rate as GDP since 1979. There has been an increasing penetration of truck freight, which has grown by more than 11 per cent per annum since 1984 compared with growth in rail freight of slightly under 6 per cent per annum. The share of truck freight increased from just under 10 per cent to 13.3 per cent between 1984 and 1993, while the railway's share in total freight traffic fell from 46 per cent to 39.6 per cent over the same period.

As the truck fleet grows rapidly and the share of new and more efficient trucks becomes dominant, efficiency improvements are likely to be significant. Between 1985

Table 6. **Traffic volume by mode**

	1981	1993	2000	2010
Passenger kilometres (billion)	250	785	1 368	2 605
of which:				
Road	84	370	689	1 433
Air	5	48	111	301
Freight tonne kilometres (billion)	1 214	3 051	5 416	10 012
of which:				
Road	78	407	983	2 503
Railway	571	1 195	2 007	3 404

Source: ZGTJNJ, 1994; IEA projections.

and 1992, efficiency in terms of vehicle kilometres has deteriorated somewhat, reflecting an increase in truck size. A large proportion of the current truck fleet is less than 5 tonnes. However, the fuel required per tonne kilometre has declined substantially for gasoline vehicles, from 7.7 to 6.9 litres, and for diesel vehicles, from 5.3 to 4.5 litres per 100 tonne kilometre. For a variety of reasons, freight in China is carried predominantly by gasoline-driven trucks. As diesel trucks, which are now officially encouraged, are 20 to 30 per cent more efficient than gasoline trucks, efficiency is likely to receive a further boost from the shift towards diesel. The freight transportation efficiency is expected to improve by 3 per cent per annum, in fuel use per tonne kilometre.

The overall energy demand for road transportation is projected to increase from 40 Mtoe in 1993 to around 120 Mtoe by 2010. This corresponds to an annual growth rate of around 7 per cent.[9] Due to the unavailability of statistics, it is not possible to determine the precise division of this large increase between diesel and gasoline. Despite the assumed large-scale shift toward diesel vehicles, gasoline is likely to maintain a larger share throughout the period due to its current overwhelming position.

Rail transportation

The railways are a very important mode of transportation in China, as well as a major energy-consuming sector; 1993 consumption was estimated at close to one-third of the total for transportation. The bulk of this was accounted for by coal used by steam engines, although there has been a very sharp increase in locomotives not powered by coal during the past twelve years. Indeed, China is reported to have stopped manufacturing coal-fired steam locomotives, the use of which could be effectively eliminated within the next ten years. However, growing oil demand – especially for other transportation needs – and uncertainty regarding the availability of domestic oil supplies may lead to more emphasis on electrification, at least for the most intensively used part of the rail network. Currently, about 10 per cent of the 54 000 kilometres of rail track in China accounts for 40 per cent of the total tonne kilometres transported. Already, 9 000 kilometres of track are electrified. The shift towards diesel and electric locomotives, while increasing the demand for scarce fuel sources, is likely to result in much more efficient rail transportation, coal being nearly four times less energy-efficient. It is assumed that coal use in rail transportation will be gradually eliminated by 2003.

It is estimated that around 40 per cent of railway freight is accounted for by the requirements for coal transportation. Conversely, nearly 70 per cent of China's coal production is distributed by rail. Thus, the future trends in railway traffic will depend strongly on coal transportation requirements which, in turn, will depend on: *a)* the total production of coal, *b)* the proportion of coal likely to be used by minemouth power stations, the construction of which is a declared policy goal, and *c)* the proportion of coal-washing, which is currently limited to 20 per cent. These factors, together with capacity increases in the railway network, will very much determine the available rail capacity for other freight. The projections here are based on the assumption that the proportion of coal-washing increases and that the dependence of coal production on rail transportation will decline from 70 per cent to 50 per cent by 2010, as greater emphasis is placed on minemouth power generation. Road freight is likely to be required to cover any shortfalls in rail capacity.

Air transportation

The most spectacular growth in passenger kilometres has been in aviation travel, which grew by nearly 21 per cent per annum between 1978 and 1993. Despite this, the share of air travel in total transport was just 6 per cent in 1993, very low for a country of China's geographical size. Air travel is expected to grow at 160 per cent of the rate of growth of the economy over the outlook period, a significant decrease from the trend in the 1980s. Given that load factors are, reportedly, already very high and that a large part of the fleet is likely to be new, efficiency improvement for the period to 2010 has been assumed to be 2 per cent per annum. Aviation fuel demand is projected to grow by 8.6 per cent per annum until 2010, a fraction of growth rates experienced in recent years.

Total transport demand projections

Oil demand in the transport sector is projected to grow by close to 7 per cent per annum over the outlook period. By the year 2010, China is assumed to use only oil products and some electricity in the transport sector, as the use of coal is phased out entirely. This assumption may be somewhat optimistic given that in 1993 coal accounted for 21 per cent of total transport energy demand.

It is also important to note that water transport, which includes river and ocean transport, accounts for a very large proportion of China's freight, and is likely to continue to play a significant role in total freight transportation.

Other energy demand

Agricultural energy demand, which accounts for over 6 per cent of commercial total final consumption, grew by only 3.1 per cent per annum between 1983 and 1993, much

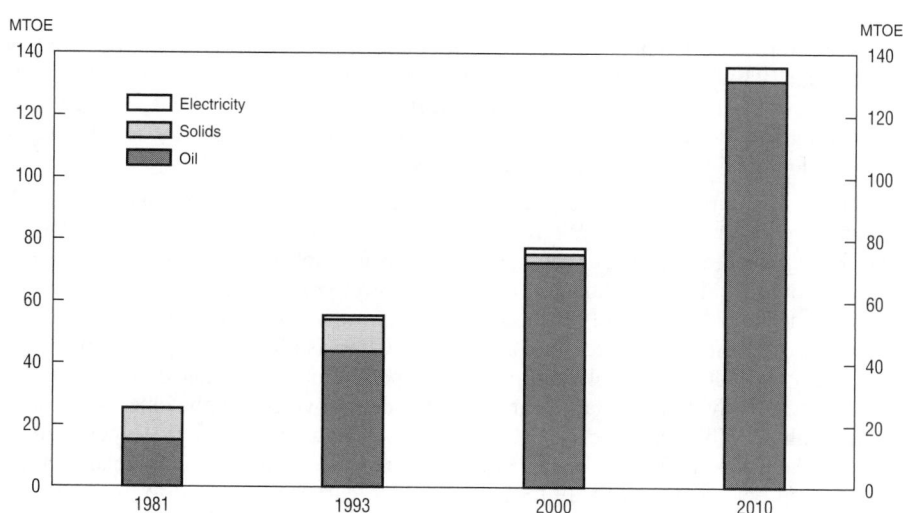

Figure 6. **Energy demand in transport by fuel**

MTOE

- ☐ Electricity
- ▨ Solids
- ▣ Oil

1981   1993   2000   2010

Source: IEA.

less than overall energy demand and the economy as a whole. In the period to 2010, agricultural energy demand is projected to increase by around 2 per cent per annum, only half the rate of growth in overall agricultural GDP. Part of the reason for the modest energy demand growth is the gradual shift towards more efficient machinery that uses oil and electricity rather than coal. These projections could, however, prove conservative. Significantly, the growth of energy demand in this sector has lagged far behind growth in the consumption capacity of installed agricultural machinery, suggesting substantial rationing. Indeed, it has been estimated that 70 per cent of agricultural oil-using machinery can work for only 160 hours per year (Asian Development Bank, 1991). Thus, there could be a substantial amount of suppressed demand in the sector that is likely to materialise as fuel availability improves. Also, rising farm incomes and the expected increase in township and village enterprises may provide a further impetus to the mechanisation of agriculture. This mechanisation process may become necessary as agricultural land becomes increasingly scarce and depleted from the intensive use of manufactured fertilizers.

Non-energy use consists mostly of oil products, such as bitumen and lubricants, and accounted for nearly 7 per cent of total final oil consumption in 1993. It is projected to grow broadly in line with total final consumption of oil.

113

IV. Electricity and heat generation

According to official data, electricity demand grew by close to 13 per cent per annum from 1949 to 1989, with the growth rate remaining close to that of GDP over the past five years. In 1989, 75 per cent of final electricity consumption was accounted for by industry, indicating both the importance of industry for China's energy system and the underdevelopment of the residential and commercial sector.

The per capita electricity consumption in rural areas in 1991 amounted to 14 kWh per annum, compared with 67 kWh for urban areas (Asian Development Bank, 1991). (In South Korea, in comparison, per capita electricity consumption in the residential sector as a whole is over 500 kWh per annum.) Growth in power generation has not kept pace with electricity demand, and severe power shortages are very common. Factories have been known to close for lack of power, and daily life in China is often interrupted by blackouts. The current gap between supply and demand at peak times is estimated at around 10 to 15 GW. There is, however, a large variation between provinces, with some experiencing few difficulties. China's electricity demand is expected to grow by 5.7 per cent per annum in the period to 2010. The fast growth in the residential and commercial sector, at 10.3 per cent per annum, is likely to make the load curve steeper and to exacerbate the shortages at peak times unless capacity can increase significantly faster than overall demand.

Figure 7. **Electricity demand by sector**

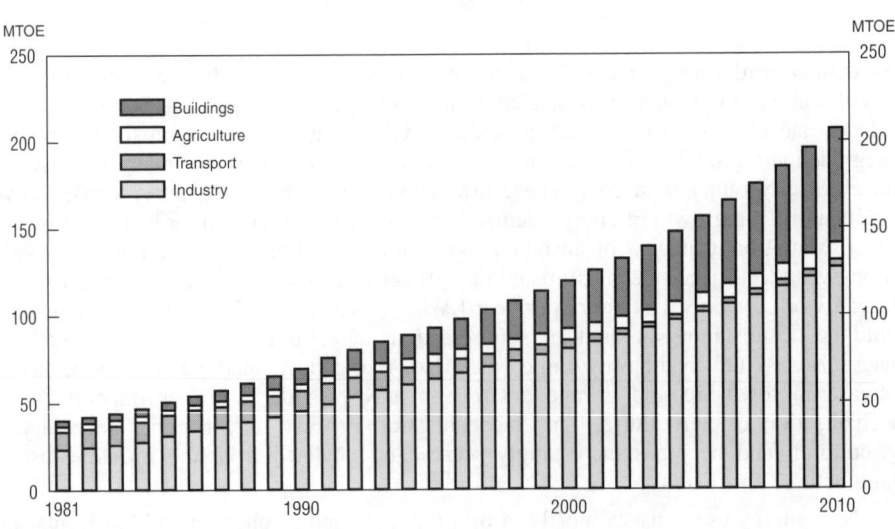

Source: IEA.

In 1993, around 82 per cent of electricity was generated from thermal – mostly coal-fired – plants, while 18.1 per cent was hydroelectric. The end-1993 power-generating capacity in China was 175 GW and included around 44 GW of hydroelectric, just under 115 GW of coal, 9 GW of oil and very little gas. The projections presented here include an overall increase in capacity of 86 GW by 2000 and around 266 GW by 2010. While these projections may appear high, they must be seen in the context of China's very rapid recent increases in capacity. Almost 60 GW was built over the past five years, and according to revised plans an average of up to 17 GW could be built annually over the rest of the decade. Capacity by 2000 is now officially projected at 285 to 300 GW (producing 1 300 to 1 350 TWh), more than double the 1990 level and compared with 230 GW planned as recently as two years ago. The experience and projections of some provinces are even more impressive. For example, in the Guangdong Province, capacity has increased from less than 3 GW in 1981 to more than 11 GW now, and a tremendous increase is projected by 2010. Thus, the projections here tend to be conservative, and based on fairly optimistic assumptions regarding efficiency and heat co-production.

The investment requirements for this expansion are likely to be very high. Even using domestically produced equipment, a 1 kW increase in coal-fired capacity costs approximately 4 000 yuan (100 fen = 1 yuan = 0.17 US dollar), with the cost being much higher for imported equipment. China currently manufactures 300 MW units, but 600 MW units are now planned. Current manufacturing capacity is 10 GW per year, implying that a significant amount of equipment will need to be imported. The overall cost of electricity produced is close to 30 fen per kWh for a new baseload coal plant and slightly higher for hydroelectric. This comparison is clearly dependent on the assumed interest rate, hydrological conditions and the price of coal. Operating costs are from 5 to 7 fen for hydroelectric and from 12 to 14 fen for coal plant at a cost of 200 yuan per tonne of fuel. For many classes of consumers, electricity tariffs are lower than costs, although tariffs have been rising in recent years.

Thermal power generation

Despite the very rapid growth of nuclear and hydro power generation, China's electricity is expected to continue to be dominated by coal-fired plant. Coal capacity is projected to increase to more than 174 GW by 2000 and to 293 GW by 2010. Due to transportation problems arising from the disparity between the locations of supply and demand for coal in China, there is a policy emphasis on locating power plants near coal mines, and transporting the electricity rather than the coal.

No significant expansion of oil-fired capacity is projected, due to the expected shortage of oil in China. Official policy discourages the use of oil in power generation, and there is some discussion about converting current oil plants to coal. However, regions like Guangdong (where a very large proportion of China's oil-fired capacity is based) that depend on coal of moderate quality obtained from a very long distance may increase their oil capacity. Also, if the problem of peak shortages is adequately addressed, more oil-based plants may be built. However, no growth is expected in overall oil-fired capacity, which is projected to remain at its 1993 level of 9 GW.

Gas-based capacity is projected to remain marginal in China's power generation system, although it is assumed that capacity expands from less than 1 GW to 3 GW by 2010 due to some new plants in coastal areas. If recent discussions on LNG projects proceed well, combined-cycle gas plants in coastal regions could expand capacity by even more than is assumed here.

If heat co-generation is excluded, efficiency of electricity generation in China is quite low. Major problems include the small scale of facilities, inconsistent coal quality and, often, low load factors due to lack of fuel. Only 12 per cent of power-generating units are 300 MW or more, compared with 60 to 80 per cent in OECD countries. In fact, more than one-fifth of the total thermal capacity in China consists of small power-generating plants. These generate less than 50 MW of electricity and are very inefficient in terms of both cost containment and power maximisation. Environmental restrictions are very weak in many of them, and emissions per kWh are much higher than the emission levels associated with larger plants. However, these small plants do have the major advantage of being easy to build and have provided a quick energy source to deal with the persistent problem of shortages. In the current eighth five-year plan, some 5.5 GW of these very-low-efficiency plants will be replaced by larger 8 GW units with the same site and fuel specifications.

If heat co-generation is included, the overall efficiency of the power-generating system in China is quite high, averaging 45 per cent in 1993. In 1993 heat accounted for 22 per cent of total generation in terms of million tonnes of oil equivalent. The Asian Development Bank reported current plans in China to build a further 10 GW of co-generation plants. There is likely to be a decline in the overall efficiency of the system if this capacity is not increased further. New regulations encourage co-generation for power plants which are at least 100 MW and operate at least 4 000 hours per year. In the projections, the 1993 proportion of heat co-generation is expected – perhaps somewhat optimistically – to stay the same until 2010.

Table 7. **Projections of gross power generation in China**

Gigawatts

	1985	1993	2000	2010
Thermal	60.7	131.2	185.9	304.2
Hydro	26.4	43.1	70.4	123.7
Nuclear	0	0.3	3.1	10.7
Total	87.1	174.5	259.4	438.6

Source: 1985 from Ministry of Energy, 1992; 1993, 2000 and 2010 from IEA.

Own use and distribution losses

Data for 1993 indicate that almost 16 per cent of power generated was used in power station consumption or lost in transmission and distribution, before reaching the consumer. These losses may be difficult to reduce, given both China's extensive rural network, where losses can amount to 30 per cent, and the financial constraints for installing high-efficiency transformers (Meyers *et al.*, 1993). It should be noted, however, that when heat and power are combined, the overall system losses in 1993 amounted to just under 13 per cent.

V. Energy resources and supply

China is well endowed with energy resources, especially hydrological potential and coal reserves. Unfortunately, there is a mismatch between the location of the resource and the location of consumption for both of these fuels. More than three-quarters of existing coal reserves are concentrated in the north and northwest of the country, far from the large consuming centres in the eastern part. Similarly, hydro resources are mainly concentrated in the western part of China. This necessitates the transportation of an immense amount of coal or electricity for distances of up to 3 000 kilometres, making transportation and energy bottlenecks highly interdependent.

Coal

According to national estimates, China's coal resources to a depth of 2 kilometres amounted to 4 500 billion tonnes, and the total proven reserves in 1991 were close to 1 000 billion tonnes (Ministry of Energy, 1992). Bituminous coal accounted for 75 per cent and anthracite for 12 per cent. China is the biggest consumer of solids in the world, as well as the most coal-intensive among the major countries. China's production of solids grew by around 5 per cent from 1980 to 1993, reaching a total of over 1 150 million tonnes in 1993. Official plans projected coal production rising by 40 million tonnes per year to reach around 1 400 million tonnes by 2000. In this outlook, growth in primary coal demand, at over 3 per cent per annum, would lead to an overall demand of 950 Mtoe, equivalent to the total thermal content of more than 1 500 million tonnes in 1991. Meeting this demand is unlikely to present severe problems, given the increasingly large proportion of coal available to producers at a market price. In fact, coal production is expected to rise at a rate similar to primary demand and no significant increase in exports is projected over the outlook period. Coal exports exceeded 24 million tonnes in 1994, more than three times their level over the preceding decade. While China's export supply capacity could increase from the current level, the strong domestic pressures on demand and the already overburdened transportation system are unlikely to allow Chinese net exports to rise much above recent levels.

China's massive coal industry is currently undergoing large changes as the traditional dominance of the state sector gradually declines. Nearly 45 per cent of coal comes from 600 centrally controlled mines, and the remaining 55 per cent comes from

80 000 mines owned by local or collective groups (Ministry of Energy, 1992). These locally controlled mines were responsible for a large part of the expansion in the 1980s (Albouy, 1991), but they are chronically unsafe and too small to support investment in washing and other high technology equipment.

Less than 20 per cent of coal in China was washed in 1991. Since unwashed coal requires more space in transit, increasing the proportion of washed coal (at a reported cost of 15 yuan per tonne) could reduce transport requirements by more than 10 per cent per annum. Coal transportation already accounts for 40 per cent of rail tonnage. High subsidisation of rail transportation leads to the underutilisation of less-energy-intensive water transportation (Albouy, 1991). In addition to the reduction in transport requirements, the use of washed coal would also reduce the level of ash in coal-processing. Unfortunately, the potential for washing is limited by the scarcity of water in many coal-producing areas and by the lack of equipment in the fast-growing local small-mine sector. Also, the price differential between washed and unwashed coal may be too high for users to prefer washed coal.

Oil

Oil production

China has only recently become a major oil producer, with its production climbing from around 0.5 million barrels per day in 1970 to close to 2.9 million barrels per day in 1994. Nearly 40 per cent of the current production comes from the Daqing field. This field is now fully mature and its production is held at a level above 1 million barrels per day through quite extensive secondary oil recovery methods. However, as Daqing's production capability inevitably declines, increased production from other fields, such as Shengli, the second-largest producing field, is likely to maintain Chinese oil production on a modest upward trend throughout the 1990s. The level of production is expected to be around 3 million barrels per day by 1995 and slightly over 3 million barrels per day by 2000. This increase in production is negligible when compared with that of oil consumption, which is projected to grow from 2.7 million barrels per day in 1992 to 4 million barrels per day by 2000. Thus, China gradually became an oil importer in early 1990s and had to import oil amounting to 500 kb/d in May 1995. Consequently, it is expected that the economy will become an increasingly significant importer by the second half of 1990s. In this context, it is also important to observe the shift in sources of Chinese crude imports. While before 1992 China's oil imports primarily came from the Asia-Pacific region, since 1993 that volume has been exceeded by crude imports from the Middle East. The expected increase of oil imports from the Middle East region makes China a more important player in the world oil trade.

The bulk of oil production during the 1990s is likely to continue to come from onshore areas, given the rather disappointing results of significant offshore exploration in the 1980s by Chinese and foreign companies. While the success rate of offshore drilling has been high and many substantial deposits have been discovered, including some with more than 1 billion barrels, the position and nature of these deposits permits only small productive flows. Thus, Chinese offshore production is unlikely to exceed 0.2 million barrels per day by 1995. From 1984 to 1992, spending by overseas companies, mostly involved in offshore exploration, declined 40 per cent. To reverse this trend, the Chinese Government adopted more favourable terms for foreign companies in 1989. However, the impact of this policy is still uncertain.

While there are many unexplored and promising areas in China, its longer-term oil production outlook depends to a large extent on the true geologic potential and timing of development of the Tarim basin. This basin has been recognised as one of the most potentially productive in the world for many years but its exploration and development have been very slow. This is due partly to the remoteness and extremely hostile conditions of the region and partly to the Chinese Government's unwillingness, until recently, to allow foreign participation. Estimates of potential reserves in the Tarim basin vary from as little as a few billion barrels to upwards of 30 billion barrels. Given rapidly growing oil needs, development of this basin is essential if China is to achieve a high level of oil self-sufficiency in the future.

In the 1991-95 budget a significant portion of the exploration budget is to be used for further exploration in the Tarim basin. In early 1993 there was already a major strike in central Tarim with 0.7 billion barrels. However, because of its remoteness, the very high cost of full development, and the need for a pipeline to eastern China, the full development of Tarim could only be undertaken if sufficient reserves were proven to sustain production of at least 0.5 to 1.0 million barrels per day. At the beginning of 1993 the government opened up parts of the basin to foreign companies and even before the closing of the bidding, more than 60 companies had expressed interest in participation. One of the factors that need to be taken into account is that, based on the current rate of increase in crude oil production costs, the average cost of Chinese crude oil by 1998 will reach or surpass international oil prices.[10]

The cost of the pipeline from the Tarim basin to eastern China, which would be the longest pipeline in the world, could be around $10 billion. It is doubtful that without foreign participation Tarim would be fully developed before 2010. In this study it is assumed that oil production in China rises to around 4 million barrels per day by 2010; most of the increase from the level reached in the year 2000 (just under 1 million barrels per day) is assumed to originate from Tarim. Depending on the degree of opening up of

Table 8. **Oil consumption and supply**

Million barrels per day

	1992	2000	2010
Consumption	2.7	4.0	6.4
Supply	2.8	3.2	3.6
Net imports	0.1	0.8	2.8

Source: IEA.

the region and the success of exploration, total oil production in China could reach 5 million barrels per day by 2010, limiting its net oil imports to 1.3 million barrels per day.

Oil refining

Until the late 1980s, the Chinese refining industry was largely isolated from international markets. It has grown at a remarkable pace since 1960 in order to supply products to the internal markets by processing China's predominantly heavy, waxy, low-sulphur crudes. With the exception of a relatively small flow of surplus gasoline, reflecting the dominance of catalytic cracking among the secondary conversion processes, there was very little international trade in petroleum products. As domestic crude production began to stagnate in the late 1980s at 2.7 to 2.8 million barrels per day against a background of rapidly growing internal product demand, the government allowed the import of petroleum products in 1986. Later, in 1988, it sanctioned the import of crude oil for the first time since the Sino-Soviet split in 1960.

Imports of petroleum products have risen significantly in recent years to meet rising demand in the southern provinces. These provinces are in structural deficit in all main fuel categories since refineries were located close to producing fields in the northeast and eastern provinces. For the first time in recent history, China emerged as a net importer of finished products in 1992. Rapid demand growth in recent years has exposed the long-standing regional imbalances. Additionally, the disproportionate growth of diesel use in transport, industry and power generation has highlighted the orientation of existing refineries towards production of gasoline rather than other transportation fuels.

Refining capacity and utilisation in China have historically matched the evolution of domestic oil use. This reflects, of course, the supply-side constraints to energy use which were evident until recent moves to liberalise trade. In 1994, distillation capacity was 3.4 million barrels per day – 90 per cent of which is controlled by the China National Petrochemical Corporation, set up in 1983. It is estimated that this capacity amounts to 3.5 million barrels per day in 1995. Crude throughputs in 1994 were 2.5 million barrels per day. The process design of almost all Chinese refineries means that very few plants are at present capable of handling high-sulphur imported crude. By the year 2000, a further 0.8 million barrels per day of capacity is likely to be built in view of projected demand growth and extensive interest from potential foreign investors. New capacity will be oriented heavily toward the processing of sour imported crude and the production of high-quality distillate products.

Some of the incremental distillation, conversion and distillation capacity in the years to 2000 is expected to come from expansion at existing refinery sites in view of the high capital cost of "greenfield" developments. Although refining industry expansion is expected to ensure that China remains broadly balanced in oil products, continuing regional and output mix imbalances may lead to a further expansion of international trade.

Gas

While natural gas production in China grew strongly throughout the 1960s and 1970s with the discovery of large fields in Sichuan Province, it remains a marginal fuel within the vast Chinese energy system. In recent years, gas has suffered from production cutbacks, and current production levels are low relative to the potential reserves base and to current oil production levels. Currently, over 50 per cent of natural gas is consumed in oilfield uses, such as for the heating of crude for pipelines and for re-injection, which may account for its low usage in other sectors of the economy.

VI. Energy issues

Trends in energy intensity[11]

China's energy intensity would be expected to be comparatively high for a multitude of reasons:
- The share of industry in the economy is quite high compared with other countries, and much of the industry is characterised by low value-added.
- A large portion of industry is inefficient because of its small scale.
- The wasteful use of materials, as well as the presence of old and inefficient technologies, results in the squandering of energy resources.
- The fuel mix in China is heavily weighted towards coal, which tends to have efficiency penalties (in the residential sector, for example, new coal stoves have 20 to 30 per cent efficiency ratings compared with 40 per cent for kerosene and 50 to 60 per cent for LPG and gas).
- Low energy prices provide few incentives for saving energy.
- And finally, energy is, to a large extent, inefficiently produced, especially in the power generation sector where large production losses are common.

There is a danger, however, of exaggerating the level of energy intensity in China and other developing countries due to many definitional and measurement problems. For example, if GNP in 1987 US dollars at standard exchange rates is used, China would appear to have an extremely high intensity in 1993 of 1.33 kgoe per US dollar, compared with less than 0.2 in Japan, about 0.4 in the United States and 0.62 in India. If, on the other hand, purchasing power parity is used to convert yuan to dollars, China's energy intensity, at 0.38 kgoe per US dollar, appears to be quite low, certainly when compared with the United States. These results are highly sensitive to the year of comparison and to exchange rates. It is probably reasonable to argue that these numbers should be seen as two extremes, and that China is a fairly energy-intensive country but not as intensive as would be implied from a superficial look at the numbers using current exchange rates.

Whatever China's true energy intensity, the apparent commercial energy intensity decline of around 4 per cent per annum from 1983 to 1993 is very impressive, if not unique. (It should be noted that if non-commercial fuels are included, the decline in intensity is even greater.) It is quite common for developing countries to have a stable or rising energy intensity as they industrialise. To the extent that the declining trend in energy intensity is accurate and not due to special characteristics of China, it could provide very useful insights to other developing countries, such as India, on ways to limit both energy needs and environmental consequences without jeopardising their growth prospects.

The possibility exists that GDP may have been overstated in recent years, leading to an exaggeration of the improvement in energy intensity. The overstatement of growth could be the result of some double-counting of value-added and the occasional reporting of nominal values as real by some non-state enterprises. A further major reason for the decline in energy intensity over the 1980-85 period was the sharp increase of imported embodied energy, especially in the form of steel. Steel imports rose from under 5 million tons in 1981 to more than 25 million tons in 1985. This trend was reversed in the 1985-90 period, but could be reversed yet again in the 1990s as the Chinese economy becomes more open.

Given the importance of industry in China's overall demand for energy and the better quality of industrial statistics, it is useful to examine the intensity issue in the context of industrial intensity trends. In terms of overall industry statistics, China's performance is even more impressive. Between 1983 and 1993, China's industrial energy demand grew by 4.8 per cent while its industrial output grew by about 13 per cent, an intensity improvement of around 8 per cent per annum. These numbers are clearly dependent on the degree of sectoral disaggregation.[12] Perhaps the most important question is the extent to which this impressive performance has been due to structural change (something that may be difficult for other countries to follow) or to technological efficiency improvements.

The contrast between Table 9 and Table 10 is quite marked, and indicates that there is a danger of overestimating the technological efficiency impact. Table 10, where intensity is defined in natural units, shows that the pure efficiency gains are likely to have been of the order of 1 to 2 per cent per year. While this rate of efficiency improvement is quite impressive, it is only a fraction of what is indicated by Table 9, where intensity improvements are defined in value terms. The natural units of Table 10 avoid many problems associated with value calculations, which may be especially difficult in the case of China. The much higher improvements indicated by Table 9 are also likely to be due

Table 9. **Industrial energy intensity changes**

Based on tce/million 1980 yuan

	1985	1990	% p.a.
Metallurgy	1 740	1 540	2.4
Chemicals	1 433	1 026	6.5
Building materials	1 627	1 074	8.0

Source: World Bank, 1993.

Table 10.

Table 10. **Industrial energy intensity changes based on natural units**

Tce/tonne

	1980	1990	% p.a.	Developed countries
Steel[a]	1.2	1.0	1.8	0.65-0.85
Cement[b]	0.207	0.188	1.1	0.12-0.13
Ammonia[c]	1.53	1.36	1.5	1.00-1.15

a) Crude steel comparable consumption (all plants rate is –2.3 per cent).
b) 1980-89 large and medium plants (small plant rate is 0.6 per cent).
c) Large plants.
Source: World Bank, 1993.

partly to the quality changes as well as structural changes within the subsectors towards higher-value-added products. The last column of Table 10 also gives some idea of the scope for improvement in new plants. Given the scarcity of capital, it is most unlikely that China will have sufficient capital resources to retro-fit or scrap old equipment.

The overall conclusion driving the projections in this outlook is that while China's energy efficiency improvements in the 1980s have been impressive, they only account for a modest proportion of the overall improvement in energy intensity. Perhaps a more important reason for such improvements is the very particular situation that China was in at the beginning of the reforms in the late 1970s. At that time, China was characterised by a relatively developed infrastructure, given the previous emphasis on energy-intensive industries, and by the absence of a well-developed consumer-oriented industry. Thus there was relatively large scope for improvement in energy intensity. The implication is that improvements in energy intensity on China's scale may be difficult to repeat in other developing countries.

Energy prices

Energy prices in China are to varying degrees controlled by the government, and significantly lower than international prices. Similarly, almost all fuel prices, particularly electricity prices, are well below their economic costs (Binsheng and Dorian, 1995; World Bank, 1994a). Since the early 1980s, the Chinese Government has introduced different measures to reform the energy pricing mechanism. However, these efforts were limited in scale (Wu and Binsheng, 1995). It is estimated that government subsidies to consumers are in the range of $16 billion annually.[13]

In 1993, as a result of the efforts to move towards a market-oriented economy, oil prices were deregulated. A subsidy phase-out policy for petroleum products – except for the agriculture sector and military use – was introduced. The proportion of market-priced petroleum products grew substantially, from about 10 per cent in 1983 to about 65 per cent in 1993 (Wang, 1995). However, on 1 May 1994 the new pricing policy was reversed and the government reimposed central control on oil prices. After experiencing a

Table 11. **Electricity tariffs for typical consumers, 1993/94**

US cents per kWh

	Average residential	Average industry
Thailand (Bangkok)	5.4	7.0
Vietnam (Hanoi)	4.3	4.3
Indonesia (Jakarta)	8.5	6.1
Korea (Seoul)	8.7	4.7
India (Bombay)	4.1	7.8
China (Beijing)	2.5	2.4
Japan	16.7	23.7

Source: World Bank, 1994c; Binsheng and Dorian, 1995; OECD/IEA (1995).

two-tiered price system for some years, the government eliminated the price regulations on coal in 1994. However, state controls on coal transportation facilities and costs still remain (Wu and Binsheng, 1995). The electricity tariff is significantly low and cannot cover the overall costs. As shown in Table 11, electricity tariffs in China, both for residential and industrial consumers, are considerably below levels internationally and in the Asian region. This low level of tariffs can impose serious barriers to the new investments required for the expansion of power generation capacity. Thus, such a pricing policy, in turn, can exacerbate the ongoing problem of power shortages.

The continuing efforts of the Chinese Government to reform energy prices are of crucial importance for the energy sector overall. As discussed above, administered energy prices lead to inefficient allocation. A market-based pricing system will improve energy conservation efforts and thus lower emission levels by creating proper incentives for enterprise energy managers.

Environmental implications

China's reliance on coal for most of its energy needs has dramatic implications for both its own and the world's environment. China is a major contributor to world carbon emissions, and it is estimated that more than 80 per cent of China's carbon emissions come from energy consumption (World Bank, 1994b). China's carbon emissions in 1993 accounted for 12.6 per cent of world emissions, as compared with 5 per cent in 1971. Though some improvement is expected in the growth rate of carbon emissions, from over 5 per cent in the period 1971-93 to less than 4 per cent from 1991 to 2010, China is still projected to emit close to 4 970 million tonnes of carbon dioxide in 2010.

Both the inefficient use of coal and its high carbon content have led to China having the highest levels of sulphur dioxide and particulates in the world. Airborne levels of sulphur dioxide exceed World Health Organization guidelines in winter, and particulate levels exceed guidelines in both winter and summer. As discussed in the first part of this outlook, under the presented economic growth assumptions, China's contribution to world emission levels is likely to continue to be extensive.

Although most of China's coal supply is located in the remote northern and western provinces, pollution concentrations are highest along the populous east coast. For example, almost 45 per cent of the sulphur dioxide emissions occur on the east coast from Liaoning Province to Shanghai, an area comprising only 8 per cent of total land in China (Yanaka and Hattori, 1992). The reason for this disparity is that most power generation facilities are located on China's heavily industrialised east coast, not at the minemouth. Building power generation facilities at the minemouth may not result in emission reductions for the country as a whole, but would do much to improve living standards for most Chinese located in urban areas.

China's environmental challenges pervade every sector of the economy. In the residential and commercial sector, coal is used for both cooking and heating, resulting in high levels of smoke in urban areas. In the rural areas, the use of fuelwood has led to severe deforestation and soil erosion. It is estimated that 180 million tons of firewood and 230 million tons of straw are burned every year (Longhai and Lujon, 1991). In the industrial sector, the prevalence of small inefficient boilers, as well as small plants in general, leads to coal waste. Emissions from urban transportation are likely to prove a major challenge over the projection period, as these have already begun to rise rapidly in several Chinese cities. In the electricity-generating sector, large quantities of fly ash are emitted as a result of outdated dust-collecting equipment and poor-quality coal.

The Chinese Government has paid particular attention to improving the environment over the last decade. From a negligible amount in 1982, investment in pollution prevention and control had increased to almost 1 per cent of national income in 1988. Policies have focused on energy conservation achieved through new and cleaner technologies.

Notes

1. This report draws on much published and unpublished work on China, as well as on discussions with experts at Lawrence Berkeley Laboratory, the World Bank, the Japanese Institute of Energy Economics, the Japan-China Association of Economy and Trade, and the following organisations within the People's Republic of China: the Energy Research Institute, the State Planning Commission, Tsingua University, the Ministry of Electric Power, the State Energy Investment Corporation, the Institute of Comprehensive Transportation, Shenergy and the Shanghai Planning Commission.

2. From *The Economist,* 15 May 1993.

3. For example, the very likely sharp end-use energy price changes have not been analysed properly since price elasticities in China cannot be obtained from historical experience. It is not clear that cross-sectional parameters would be suitable, since China's energy trends do not seem to fit the pattern of other developing countries.

4. From the *Financial Times,* 5 October 1995.

5. In discussing the overall economy and its sectoral division, the standard GNP accounting methodology has been used. It should be noted that very often, conceptually different measures are used in discussing the Chinese economy. These alternative measures and their differences are discussed in *China Energy Databook,* Lawrence Berkeley Laboratory, Chapter IX.

6. For example, in Shanghai the share of services in GNP rose from 18.6 per cent in 1978 to nearly 35 per cent in 1993.

7. Unless otherwise stated, all numbers are based on IEA conventions and exclude non-commercial fuels which are of especial significance for China.

8. However, it is important to note that due to the methodology of data collection in China, the official numbers on oil consumption by the transportation sector, as reported by the IEA, are very likely to be underestimated. Thus the projections may also prove conservative, as the starting value for this fast-growing sector may be too low.

9. It should be noted that the 1991 estimate of oil consumption in the transportation sector is very likely to be an underestimate. If this is the case, the growth in absolute terms could be much bigger.

10. Similarly, the cost of utilising domestic coal for electricity generation is expected to approach international levels when transportation and environmental costs are taken into account (*China Petroleum Newsletter,* 8 November 1995).

11. Because of the importance of the issue, much research has already been carried out on energy intensity in China. See, for example, Jiang (1992), Levine *et al.* (1992), Sinton and Levine (1993), Ying and Zhenguo (1993) and World Bank (1993).

12. Sinton and Levine (1993) examine industrial energy intensity at quite a disaggregated level.

13. In disaggregated terms; it is calculated that coal subsidies account for $5 055 million, gas subsidies $378 million and petroleum product subsidies $10 300 million (Larsen and Shah, 1992).

Bibliography

COMMISSARIAT A L'ÉNERGIE ATOMIQUE (1992), *Les Centrales Nucléaires dans le Monde*, Paris.

ECONOMIC AND SOCIAL COMMISSION FOR ASIA AND THE PACIFIC, UNITED NATIONS DEVELOPMENT PROGRAMME and the GOVERNMENT OF FRANCE (1991), *Sectoral Energy Demand Studies in Asia: Proceedings of a Regional Workshop*, ESCAP, Bangkok, 28-30 November 1989.

THE ENERGY DATA AND MODELING CENTRE (1993), *Energy and Economics Databook*, Tokyo.

IEA, *Oil Market Report*, various issues, Paris.

IEA (1991*a*), *Energy Efficiency and the Environment*, Paris.

IEA (1991*b*), *Fuel Efficiency of Passenger Cars*, Paris.

IEA (1991*c*), *Natural Gas Prospects and Policies*, Paris.

IEA (1995*a*), *Energy Balances of OECD Countries*, Paris.

IEA (1995*b*), *Energy Policies of IEA Countries*, Paris.

IEA (1995*c*), *Coal Information*, 1994, Paris.

IEA (1995*d*), *Energy Prices and Taxes, Third Quarter 1995*, Paris.

IEA (1995*e*), *World Energy Outlook*, Paris.

IEA (1995*f*), *Energy Statistics and Balances on Non-OECD Countries*, Paris.

INTERNATIONAL IRON AND STEEL INSTITUTE, *Statistics on Energy in the Steel Market*, various issues, Brussels.

INTERNATIONAL MONETARY FUND (1995*a*), *World Economic Outlook*, Washington, DC.

INTERNATIONAL MONETARY FUND (1995*b*), *International Financial Statistics Yearbook*, Washington, DC.

JAPAN PETROCHEMICAL INDUSTRY ASSOCIATION (1993), *Petrochemical Industry of Japan*.

MASTERS, C.D., D.H. ROOT and E.D. ATTANASI (1990), "World Oil and Gas Resources: Future Production Realities", *Annual Review of Energy*.

MITSUBISHI CORPORATION (1993), *Natural Gas Situation in the Far East Toward 2010*, IEA Second Energy Experts Meeting, Paris, November.

OECD (1992), *Structural Change and Industrial Performance*, Paris.

OECD (1994*a*), *Economic Outlook*, Paris, December.

OECD (1994*b*), *National Accounts Detailed Tables*, Vol. II, Paris.

Oil and Gas Journal (1993), "World LNG Trade to Soar to 2010 if Prices, Funds Line Up", 28 June.

UNIDO [United Nations Industrial Development Organisation] (1992), *Industry and Development, Global Report,* various issues, Vienna.

UNITED NATIONS, *Statistical Yearbook,* various issues, New York.

UNITED NATIONS (1991), *Sectoral Energy Demand Studies: Application of the End-Use Approach to Asian Countries,* Energy Resources Development Series, No. 33, New York.

UNITED NATIONS (1992), *World Population Prospects 1990,* New York.

UNITED NATIONS (1993), *The Steel Market in 1992,* New York.

WORLD BANK (1992), *Market Outlook for Major Primary Commodities,* Volume 1, Report 814/92, Washington, DC, October.

China

ALBOUY, Yves (1991), "Coal Pricing in China: Issues and Reform Strategy", World Bank Discussion Papers, No. 138.

ASIAN DEVELOPMENT BANK (1991), *Environmental Considerations in Energy Development.*

ASIAN DEVELOPMENT BANK (1993), *Electric Utilities Databook for the Asian and Pacific Region.*

BINSHENG, Li and James DORIAN (1995), "Change in China's Power Sector", *Energy Policy,* Vol. 23, No. 5.

China British Trade Review, various issues.

China Petroleum Newsletter (1995), Vol. 2, No. 23, November.

The Economist (1992), "Visitors to the Middle Kingdom", 3 October, p. 57.

THE ECONOMIST INTELLIGENCE UNIT (1995), China, North Korea Country Profile.

Energy Economist (1993), "Chinese Number Games", June.

FENG, Liu (1993), *"Energy Use and Conservation in China's Residential and Commercial Sectors: Patterns, Problems, and Prospects",* Lawrence Berkeley Laboratory, July.

FENG, Liu, W.B. DAVIS and M.D. LEVINE (1992), *"An Overview of Energy Supply and Demand in China",* Lawrence Berkeley Laboratory, May.

FRIEDLEY, David (1991), *China's Energy Outlook, East West Centre,* Honolulu, Hawaii.

HUANG, Jin-Ping (1993*a*), "Electricity Consumption and Economic Growth: A Case Study for China", *Energy Policy,* June.

HUANG, Jin-Ping (1993*b*), "Energy Substitution to Reduce Carbon Dioxide Emission in China", *Energy,* Vol. 18, No. 3, pp. 281-287.

JIANG, Z. (1992), "Energy Efficiency in China", mimeo.

LANG, Siwei and Yu Joe HUANG (1993), "Energy Conservation Standard for Space Heating in Chinese Urban Residential Building", *Energy,* Vol. 18, No. 8, pp. 871-892.

LARSEN, Bjorn and Anwar SHAH (1992), "World Fossil Fuel Subsidies and Global Carbon Emissions", World Bank Policy Research Working Paper 1002.

LAWRENCE BERKELEY LABORATORY (1993), *China Energy Databook,* Berkeley, California.

LEVINE, Mark D., Liu FENG and Jonathan E. SINTON (1992), "China's Energy System: Historical Evolution, Current Issues, and Prospects", *Annual Energy Review,* Vol. 17, pp. 405-435.

LIN, Xiannuan (1992), "Declining Energy Intensity in China's Industrial Sector", *The Journal of Energy and Development,* Vol. 16, No. 2.

LONGHAI, Shen (1993), "China's Energy Situation and Energy Saving Policy" in IEA (ed.), *Proceedings of the International Conference on Energy Efficiency in Asian Countries,* Tokyo, 4-5 November 1992.

LONGHAI, Shen and Liu LUJON (1991), "Energy Development and Environmental Protection: Dual Challenges for China", *Energy and Environment,* Vol. 2, No. 4.

MEYERS, S., N. GOLDMAN, N. MARTIN and R. FRIEDMAN (1993), *"Prospects for the Power Sector in Nine Developing Countries",* Lawrence Berkeley Laboratory, April.

MINISTRY OF ENERGY, *Energy in China* (various years), People's Republic of China.

PAIK, Keun-Wook (1993), "Tarim Opening: Geopolitics of Chinese Oil", *Geopolitics of Energy,* April.

People's Republic of China Yearbook, 1989-90, Vol. 9 (1990), PRC Yearbook Ltd., Beijing.

PERLACK, D.R. and M. RUSSELL (1991), "Energy and Environmental Policy in China", *Annual Review of Energy and the Environment,* Vol. 16, pp. 205-233.

ROSS, M. and Liu FENG (1991), "The Energy Efficiency of the Steel Industry of China", *Energy,* Vol. 16, No. 5, pp. 833-848.

SATHAYE, J. and S. TYLER (1991), "Transitions in Household Energy Use in Urban China, India, the Philippines, Thailand and Hong Kong", *Annual Review of Energy and the Environment,* Vol. 16, pp. 295-335.

SINTON, E.J. and M.D. LEVINE (1993), "Changing Energy Intensity in Chinese Industry", mimeo.

UNDP (1989), *Sectoral Energy Demand in China,* Regional Energy Development Programme (RAS/86/136).

VERGARA, W. and D. BABELON (1990), "The Petrochemical Industry in Developing Asia", World Bank Technical Papers, No. 113.

WANG, Haijang (1995), "China's Oil Policy and Its Impact", *Energy Policy,* Vol. 23, No. 7.

WORLD BANK (1992), "Market Outlook for Major Primary Commodities", Volume 1, Report 814/92, Washington, DC, October.

WORLD BANK (1993), "China: Energy Conservation Study", World Bank Report No. 10813-CHA, Washington, DC, February.

WORLD BANK (1994a), "A Survey of Asia's Energy Prices", World Bank Technical Papers, No. 248, Washington, DC.

WORLD BANK (1994b), *Asia Energy Profile, Energy Sector Performance,* Asia Technical Department, Washington, DC, November.

WORLD BANK (1994c), *China: Estimation of Greenhouse Gas Emissions and Sinks in China,* Subreport No. 1, Washington, DC.

WORLD BANK (1995), *World Development Report 1995,* Washington, DC.

WU, Kang and Li BINSHENG (1995), "Energy Development in China", *Energy Policy,* Vol. 23, No. 2.

YANAKA, Yukichi and Takeshi HATTORI (1992), ''Air Pollution Problems in China and Subjects to International Cooperation'', *Energy in Japan,* No. 113, January.

YING, Shi and Yu ZHENGUO (1993), ''An Analysis of China's Energy Intensity'' in a publication of the International Association of Energy Economists, Bali, Indonesia.

ZGTJNJ (1994), *Zhongguo Tongji Nianjian* [China Statistical Yearbook], China Statistical Press, Beijing.

Annex

List of participants

Chairman

Jean-Claude PAYE
Secretary-General of the OECD

Participants

David L. AARON
Ambassador
Head of the United States
Delegation to the OECD

Howard R. BALLOCH
Deputy Secretary
Intergovernmental Affairs
Privy Council Office
Canada

Vincent CABLE
Chief Economist
Shell International
United Kingdom

Kenneth S. COURTIS
First Vice President
and Chief Economist
Deutsche Bank Capital Markets (Asia) Ltd.
Japan

Phillip CROWSON
Head of the Economics Department
RTZ Corp. Plc
United Kingdom

Michèle DEBONNEUIL (Mme)
Directeur des Études économiques
et financières
Banque Indosuez
France

Heinz DOLLBERG
Executive Vice President, Asia
Allianz Holding AG
Germany

H.J. DROST
Member of the Executive Board
Heineken N.V.
The Netherlands

FAN Gang
Deputy Director
Institute of Economics
Chinese Academy of Social Sciences
People's Republic of China

Michael GARRETT
Executive Vice President
Nestlé S.A.
Switzerland

Norbert GRAEBER
Executive Vice President
Head of the Daimler-Benz Group
Representation Office Beijing
Daimler-Benz AG
Germany

GUO Shuging
Director General
Comprehensive Department
State Commission for the Restructuring
of the Economic System
People's Republic of China

Nicholas C. HOPE
Director
China and Mongolia Department
The World Bank

Klaus-Peter KLAIBER
Director General
Ministry of Foreign Affairs
Germany

Justin Yifu LIN
Director
China Center for Economic Research
University of Beijing
People's Republic of China

LONG Yongtu
Assistant Minister
Ministry of Trade and Economic
Co-operation (MOFTEC)
People's Republic of China

Angus MADDISON
Professor of Economics
University of Groningen
The Netherlands

Wolfgang MICHALSKI
Director
Advisory Unit to the Secretary-General
OECD

Dwight H. PERKINS
Professor of Political Economy
Harvard University
United States

Robert PRIDDLE
Executive Director
International Energy Agency
OECD

Geoff RABY
Senior Advisor
Office of the Deputy Prime Minister
Australia

Christopher ROBERTS
Deputy Secretary
Department of Trade and Industry
United Kingdom

Vitor RODRIGUES PESSOA
Secretary for Economics and Finance
Macao

Shuji SHIMOKOJI
Deputy Director General
Intelligence and Analysis Bureau
Ministry of Foreign Affairs
Japan

Pietro SIGHICELLI
Vice President, International Development
FIAT Spa
Italy

John STUERMER
Vice President, Asia
The First National Bank of Chicago
United States

Veli SUNDBÄCK
Member of the Executive Board
Nokia OY
Finland

Makoto TANIGUCHI
Deputy Secretary-General
OECD

John WONG
Director
Institute of East Asian Political Economy
Singapore

Y.C. Richard WONG
Director
Hong Kong Center for Economic Research
Hong Kong

Masaru YOSHITOMI
Vice Chairman
Long-Term Credit Bank of Japan Research
Institute
Japan

WU Jinglian
Professor of Economics
Development Research Center
The State Council of the PRC
People's Republic of China

OECD Secretariat

Barrie STEVENS
Deputy Head
Advisory Unit to the Secretary-General

Riel MILLER
Advisory Unit to the Secretary-General

MAIN SALES OUTLETS OF OECD PUBLICATIONS
PRINCIPAUX POINTS DE VENTE DES PUBLICATIONS DE L'OCDE

AUSTRALIA – AUSTRALIE
D.A. Information Services
648 Whitehorse Road, P.O.B 163
Mitcham, Victoria 3132   Tel. (03) 9210.7777
     Fax: (03) 9210.7788

AUSTRIA – AUTRICHE
Gerold & Co.
Graben 31
Wien I   Tel. (0222) 533.50.14
     Fax: (0222) 512.47.31.29

BELGIUM – BELGIQUE
Jean De Lannoy
Avenue du Roi, Koningslaan 202
B-1060 Bruxelles   Tel. (02) 538.51.69/538.08.41
     Fax: (02) 538.08.41

CANADA
Renouf Publishing Company Ltd.
1294 Algoma Road
Ottawa, ON K1B 3W8   Tel. (613) 741.4333
     Fax: (613) 741.5439
Stores:
61 Sparks Street
Ottawa, ON K1P 5R1   Tel. (613) 238.8985
12 Adelaide Street West
Toronto, ON M5H 1L6   Tel. (416) 363.3171
     Fax: (416)363.59.63

Les Éditions La Liberté Inc.
3020 Chemin Sainte-Foy
Sainte-Foy, PQ G1X 3V6   Tel. (418) 658.3763
     Fax: (418) 658.3763

Federal Publications Inc.
165 University Avenue, Suite 701
Toronto, ON M5H 3B8   Tel. (416) 860.1611
     Fax: (416) 860.1608

Les Publications Fédérales
1185 Université
Montréal, QC H3B 3A7   Tel. (514) 954.1633
     Fax: (514) 954.1635

CHINA – CHINE
China National Publications Import
Export Corporation (CNPIEC)
16 Gongti E. Road, Chaoyang District
P.O. Box 88 or 50
Beijing 100704 PR   Tel. (01) 506.6688
     Fax: (01) 506.3101

CHINESE TAIPEI – TAIPEI CHINOIS
Good Faith Worldwide Int'l. Co. Ltd.
9th Floor, No. 118, Sec. 2
Chung Hsiao E. Road
Taipei   Tel. (02) 391.7396/391.7397
     Fax: (02) 394.9176

DENMARK – DANEMARK
Munksgaard Book and Subscription Service
35, Nørre Søgade, P.O. Box 2148
DK-1016 København K   Tel. (33) 12.85.70
     Fax: (33) 12.93.87

J. H. Schultz Information A/S,
Herstedvang 12,
DK – 2620 Albertslung   Tel. 43 63 23 00
     Fax: 43 63 19 69
Internet: s-info@inet.uni-c.dk

EGYPT – ÉGYPTE
Middle East Observer
41 Sherif Street
Cairo   Tel. 392.6919
     Fax: 360-6804

FINLAND – FINLANDE
Akateeminen Kirjakauppa
Keskuskatu 1, P.O. Box 128
00100 Helsinki
Subscription Services/Agence d'abonnements :
P.O. Box 23
00371 Helsinki   Tel. (358 0) 121 4416
     Fax: (358 0) 121.4450

FRANCE
OECD/OCDE
Mail Orders/Commandes par correspondance :
2, rue André-Pascal
75775 Paris Cedex 16   Tel. (33-1) 45.24.82.00
     Fax: (33-1) 49.10.42.76
     Telex: 640048 OCDE
Internet: Compte.PUBSINQ@oecd.org

Orders via Minitel, France only/
Commandes par Minitel, France exclusivement :
36 15 OCDE

OECD Bookshop/Librairie de l'OCDE :
33, rue Octave-Feuillet
75016 Paris   Tél. (33-1) 45.24.81.81
     (33-1) 45.24.81.67

Dawson
B.P. 40
91121 Palaiseau Cedex   Tel. 69.10.47.00
     Fax: 64.54.83.26

Documentation Française
29, quai Voltaire
75007 Paris   Tel. 40.15.70.00

Economica
49, rue Héricart
75015 Paris   Tel. 45.75.05.67
     Fax: 40.58.15.70

Gibert Jeune (Droit-Économie)
6, place Saint-Michel
75006 Paris   Tel. 43.25.91.19

Librairie du Commerce International
10, avenue d'Iéna
75016 Paris   Tel. 40.73.34.60

Librairie Dunod
Université Paris-Dauphine
Place du Maréchal-de-Lattre-de-Tassigny
75016 Paris   Tel. 44.05.40.13

Librairie Lavoisier
11, rue Lavoisier
75008 Paris   Tel. 42.65.39.95

Librairie des Sciences Politiques
30, rue Saint-Guillaume
75007 Paris   Tel. 45.48.36.02

P.U.F.
49, boulevard Saint-Michel
75005 Paris   Tel. 43.25.83.40

Librairie de l'Université
12a, rue Nazareth
13100 Aix-en-Provence   Tel. (16) 42.26.18.08

Documentation Française
165, rue Garibaldi
69003 Lyon   Tel. (16) 78.63.32.23

Librairie Decitre
29, place Bellecour
69002 Lyon   Tel. (16) 72.40.54.54

Librairie Sauramps
Le Triangle
34967 Montpellier Cedex 2   Tel. (16) 67.58.85.15
     Fax: (16) 67.58.27.36

A la Sorbonne Actual
23, rue de l'Hôtel-des-Postes

06000 Nice   Tel. (16) 93.13.77.75
     Fax: (16) 93.80.75.69

GERMANY – ALLEMAGNE
OECD Bonn Centre
August-Bebel-Allee 6
D-53175 Bonn   Tel. (0228) 959.120
     Fax: (0228) 959.12.17

GREECE – GRÈCE
Librairie Kauffmann
Stadiou 28
10564 Athens   Tel. (01) 32.55.321
     Fax: (01) 32.30.320

HONG-KONG
Swindon Book Co. Ltd.
Astoria Bldg. 3F
34 Ashley Road, Tsimshatsui
Kowloon, Hong Kong   Tel. 2376.2062
     Fax: 2376.0685

HUNGARY – HONGRIE
Euro Info Service
Margitsziget, Európa Ház
1138 Budapest   Tel. (1) 111.62.16
     Fax: (1) 111.60.61

ICELAND – ISLANDE
Mál Mog Menning
Laugavegi 18, Pósthólf 392
121 Reykjavik   Tel. (1) 552.4240
     Fax: (1) 562.3523

INDIA – INDE
Oxford Book and Stationery Co.
Scindia House
New Delhi 110001   Tel. (11) 331.5896/5308
     Fax: (11) 332.5993

17 Park Street
Calcutta 700016   Tel. 240832

INDONESIA – INDONÉSIE
Pdii-Lipi
P.O. Box 4298
Jakarta 12042   Tel. (21) 573.34.67
     Fax: (21) 573.34.67

IRELAND – IRLANDE
Government Supplies Agency
Publications Section
4/5 Harcourt Road
Dublin 2   Tel. 661.31.11
     Fax: 475.27.60

ISRAEL – ISRAËL
Praedicta
5 Shatner Street
P.O. Box 34030
Jerusalem 91430   Tel. (2) 52.84.90/1/2
     Fax: (2) 52.84.93

R.O.Y. International
P.O. Box 13056
Tel Aviv 61130   Tel. (3) 546 1423
     Fax: (3) 546 1442

Palestinian Authority/Middle East:
INDEX Information Services
P.O.B. 19502
Jerusalem   Tel. (2) 27.12.19
     Fax: (2) 27.16.34

ITALY – ITALIE
Libreria Commissionaria Sansoni
Via Duca di Calabria 1/1
50125 Firenze   Tel. (055) 64.54.15
     Fax: (055) 64.12.57

Via Bartolini 29
20155 Milano   Tel. (02) 36.50.83

Editrice e Libreria Herder
Piazza Montecitorio 120
00186 Roma   Tel. 679.46.28
     Fax: 678.47.51

Libreria Hoepli
Via Hoepli 5
20121 Milano   Tel. (02) 86.54.46
                                     Fax: (02) 805.28.86

Libreria Scientifica
Dott. Lucio de Biasio 'Aeiou'
Via Coronelli, 6
20146 Milano   Tel. (02) 48.95.45.52
                                     Fax: (02) 48.95.45.48

JAPAN – JAPON
OECD Tokyo Centre
Landic Akasaka Building
2-3-4 Akasaka, Minato-ku
Tokyo 107   Tel. (81.3) 3586.2016
                                     Fax: (81.3) 3584.7929

KOREA – CORÉE
Kyobo Book Centre Co. Ltd.
P.O. Box 1658, Kwang Hwa Moon
Seoul   Tel. 730.78.91
                                     Fax: 735.00.30

MALAYSIA – MALAISIE
University of Malaya Bookshop
University of Malaya
P.O. Box 1127, Jalan Pantai Baru
59700 Kuala Lumpur
Malaysia   Tel. 756.5000/756.5425
                                     Fax: 756.3246

MEXICO – MEXIQUE
OECD Mexico Centre
Edificio INFOTEC
Av. San Fernando no. 37
Col. Toriello Guerra
Tlalpan C.P. 14050
Mexico D.F.   Tel. (525) 665 47 99
                                     Fax: (525) 606 13 07

Revistas y Periodicos Internacionales S.A. de C.V.
Florencia 57 - 1004
Mexico, D.F. 06600   Tel. 207.81.00
                                     Fax: 208.39.79

NETHERLANDS – PAYS-BAS
SDU Uitgeverij Plantijnstraat
Externe Fondsen
Postbus 20014
2500 EA's-Gravenhage   Tel. (070) 37.89.880
Voor bestellingen: Fax: (070) 34.75.778

**NEW ZEALAND –
NOUVELLE-ZÉLANDE**
GPLegislation Services
P.O. Box 12418
Thorndon, Wellington   Tel. (04) 496.5655
                                     Fax: (04) 496.5698

NORWAY – NORVÈGE
NIC INFO A/S
Bertrand Narvesens vei 2
P.O. Box 6512 Etterstad
0606 Oslo 6   Tel. (022) 57.33.00
                                     Fax: (022) 68.19.01

PAKISTAN
Mirza Book Agency
65 Shahrah Quaid-E-Azam
Lahore 54000   Tel. (42) 735.36.01
                                     Fax: (42) 576.37.14

PHILIPPINE – PHILIPPINES
International Booksource Center Inc.
Rm 179/920 Cityland 10 Condo Tower 2
HV dela Costa Ext cor Valero St.
Makati Metro Manila   Tel. (632) 817 9676
                                     Fax: (632) 817 1741

POLAND – POLOGNE
Ars Polona
00-950 Warszawa
Krakowskie Przedmieácie 7   Tel. (22) 264760
                                     Fax: (22) 268673

PORTUGAL
Livraria Portugal
Rua do Carmo 70-74
Apart. 2681
1200 Lisboa   Tel. (01) 347.49.82/5
                                     Fax: (01) 347.02.64

SINGAPORE – SINGAPOUR
Gower Asia Pacific Pte Ltd.
Golden Wheel Building
41, Kallang Pudding Road, No. 04-03
Singapore 1334   Tel. 741.5166
                                     Fax: 742.9356

SPAIN – ESPAGNE
Mundi-Prensa Libros S.A.
Castelló 37, Apartado 1223
Madrid 28001   Tel. (91) 431.33.99
                                     Fax: (91) 575.39.98

Mundi-Prensa Barcelona
Consell de Cent No. 391
08009 – Barcelona   Tel. (93) 488.34.92
                                     Fax: (93) 487.76.59

Llibreria de la Generalitat
Palau Moja
Rambla dels Estudis, 118
08002 – Barcelona
                    (Subscripcions) Tel. (93) 318.80.12
                    (Publicacions) Tel. (93) 302.67.23
                                    Fax: (93) 412.18.54

SRI LANKA
Centre for Policy Research
c/o Colombo Agencies Ltd.
No. 300-304, Galle Road
Colombo 3   Tel. (1) 574240, 573551-2
                                     Fax: (1) 575394, 510711

SWEDEN – SUÈDE
CE Fritzes AB
S–106 47 Stockholm   Tel. (08) 690.90.90
                                     Fax: (08) 20.50.21

Subscription Agency/Agence d'abonnements :
Wennergren-Williams Info AB
P.O. Box 1305
171 25 Solna   Tel. (08) 705.97.50
                                     Fax: (08) 27.00.71

SWITZERLAND – SUISSE
Maditec S.A. (Books and Periodicals - Livres
et périodiques)
Chemin des Palettes 4
Case postale 266
1020 Renens VD 1   Tel. (021) 635.08.65
                                     Fax: (021) 635.07.80

Librairie Payot S.A.
4, place Pépinet
CP 3212
1002 Lausanne   Tel. (021) 320.25.11
                                     Fax: (021) 320.25.14

Librairie Unilivres
6, rue de Candolle
1205 Genève   Tel. (022) 320.26.23
                                     Fax: (022) 329.73.18

Subscription Agency/Agence d'abonnements :
Dynapresse Marketing S.A.
38, avenue Vibert
1227 Carouge   Tel. (022) 308.07.89
                                     Fax: (022) 308.07.99

See also – Voir aussi :
OECD Bonn Centre
August-Bebel-Allee 6
D-53175 Bonn (Germany)   Tel. (0228) 959.120
                                     Fax: (0228) 959.12.17

THAILAND – THAÏLANDE
Suksit Siam Co. Ltd.
113, 115 Fuang Nakhon Rd.
Opp. Wat Rajbopith
Bangkok 10200   Tel. (662) 225.9531/2
                                     Fax: (662) 222.5188

TRINIDAD & TOBAGO
SSL Systematics Studies Limited
9 Watts Street
Curepe
Trinadad & Tobago, W.I.   Tel. (1809) 645.3475
                                     Fax: (1809) 662.5654

TUNISIA – TUNISIE
Grande Librairie Spécialisée
Fendri Ali
Avenue Haffouz Imm El-Intilaka
Bloc B 1 Sfax 3000   Tel. (216-4) 296 855
                                     Fax: (216-4) 298.270

TURKEY – TURQUIE
Kültür Yayinlari Is-Türk Ltd. Sti.
Atatürk Bulvari No. 191/Kat 13
Kavaklidere/Ankara
                                     Tel. (312) 428.11.40 Ext. 2458
                                     Fax: (312) 417 24 90
Dolmabahce Cad. No. 29
Besiktas/Istanbul   Tel. (212) 260 7188

UNITED KINGDOM – ROYAUME-UNI
HMSO
Gen. enquiries   Tel. (0171) 873 0011
Postal orders only:
P.O. Box 276, London SW8 5DT
Personal Callers HMSO Bookshop
49 High Holborn, London WC1V 6HB
                                     Fax: (0171) 873 8463
Branches at: Belfast, Birmingham, Bristol,
Edinburgh, Manchester

UNITED STATES – ÉTATS-UNIS
OECD Washington Center
2001 L Street N.W., Suite 650
Washington, D.C. 20036-4922   Tel. (202) 785.6323
                                     Fax: (202) 785.0350

Internet: washcont@oecd.org

Subscriptions to OECD periodicals may also be placed
through main subscription agencies.

Les abonnements aux publications périodiques de
l'OCDE peuvent être souscrits auprès des principales
agences d'abonnement.

Orders and inquiries from countries where Distributors
have not yet been appointed should be sent to: OECD
Publications, 2, rue André-Pascal, 75775 Paris Cedex
16, France.

Les commandes provenant de pays où l'OCDE n'a pas
encore désigné de distributeur peuvent être adressées
aux Éditions de l'OCDE, 2, rue André-Pascal, 75775
Paris Cedex 16, France.

5-1996

OECD PUBLICATIONS, 2, rue André-Pascal, 75775 PARIS CEDEX 16
PRINTED IN FRANCE
(03 96 05 1) ISBN 92-64-14924-4 – No. 48853 1996